William Stringfellow a[...]

In the spring of 1[...] tracted a baffling and apparently hopeless disease which horribly wasted his body before a last-ditch operation brought about a dramatic cure. This is Stringfellow's own account of that ordeal of pain and of the fundamental beliefs that sustained him in his agony and gave him the courage to undergo the dangerous surgery that saved his life.

His vivid description of that experience, told without emotion or cant, is both startling and strengthening. His story is a personal testimony to the relevance of faith and love in the mystery of healing, and to the gift of life itself which few of us take time to recognize.

A SECOND BIRTHDAY

William
Stringfellow

A SECOND
BIRTHDAY
12798

Doubleday & Company, Inc.
Garden City, New York
1970

for
David Poling

"If I were myself an American citizen and Christian and theologian, then I would try to elaborate a theology of freedom . . . a theology of freedom . . . for—I like to say a single word—freedom for humanity . . ."

KARL BARTH

contents

A SECOND BIRTHDAY

I   ORDEAL

I am brought into so great trouble and
misery, that I go mourning all the day long.

For my loins are filled with a sore disease,
and there is no whole part in my body.

I am feeble and sore smitten; I have roared
for the very disquietness of my heart.

Psalm 38:6–8

Bengt Nordberg is to blame for this book. It was he, in the months of convalescence on Block Island, after the hospital, who became a persistent and persuasive advocate for those concerns that eventually outbalanced my qualms.

Bengt is the proprietor of a restaurant on Block Island called Smuggler's Cove, a name derived from the uses to which the premises were put during Prohibition. The Cove is a favorite and justly famous place among the summer people from New York and New England who come to the Island, but Bengt is no seasonal person and there is hospitality at Smuggler's for Island inhabitants through the winter. Bengt is not an indigenous Islander, but he is the next to that, having married a direct descendant of one of the settling families; he is a native of Sweden, spent his youth at sea, and moved years ago to Block Island because it is the place in which, as he says, he wants to die. He is a man of imposing physique, of wit worthy of a seaman, and of terrific intellectual vitality; he is expansive, gentle, generous to a fault; he is familiar with all the Island lore and a fierce partisan of the Island style of life.

the immigration

I had moved to Block Island, Rhode Island,
from New York City in the fall of 1967, together
with the poet, Anthony Towne, who had been
coauthor with me of *The Bishop Pike Affair*,
which was published about that same time, in
the midst of the so-called heresy charges that
had been leveled against Bishop Pike. Our common interests in theology and social ethics had
made Anthony and me colleagues in work as
well as friends, and our collaboration in thought
and deed extended, as it still does, far beyond
the *Pike* book. The congeniality of our thinking
on most issues is astonishing (unless one credits
the Holy Spirit); we can truly read each
other's minds. Anthony tends to be more reti-
cent, while I am more an activist, though his
thinking is more radical, both theologically and
practically, than my own. For some years, he
and I had been vaguely searching for a location outside the city, which could be used in
any season for rest and reflection and writing.
Our common household in New York had be-

come a kind of salon, to which all sorts of people came, and were welcomed, but with such
abundance and frequency that it had become
difficult to keep up with emptying the ashtrays,
much less concentrate enough to write. Thus,
we sought some circumstances in which to es-
tablish, as it were, our own monastery. There
were other considerations: some are political
and are intimated later on; another was my
health, which I had obstinately neglected so
long as I had lived in the city and which, by
1967—my eleventh year in New York—had
gradually deteriorated to such an extent that I
had received an emphatic medical admoni-
tion to get rest by establishing a different pace
somewhere outside the city. We had discovered Block Island the year before, made several visits there, become enchanted with its
moors and cliffs, been attracted by its solitude,
and decided to immigrate there.

The move from New York City seemed in
the circumstances prudent and necessary, but,
in my consciousness at least, it carried no intent
to desert the city. In this culture it is literally
impossible to flee from the city's dominance
anyway—as all those white suburbanites have
discovered—and, in my belief, the city is the
central theological symbol of society. That is
not only the contemporary reality in America,
it is the biblical insight as well. Biblically, the
city is the scene of *both* doomsday and salvation. There is Babylon, but there is also Jeru-

salem. The city is the epitome of the Fall, yet the city is the sign of the Eschaton. These connotations of death and life associated with the city empirically and theologically mean that the city cannot be escaped and that the city must not be rejected by human beings, as it seems to be by the utopian hippies and their commune movement, for example, and least of all can it be repudiated by professed Christians. (Billy Graham, if he were more attentive to the Bible, might realize this and cease his facile preaching against the city as a realm of sin and give up his proclamation of a pastoral image of salvation generally identified with the hinterland of the American South or Midwest). Coming to Block Island was not a romanticized change, and, in terms of commitment, it was no change at all. Practically, I maintained affiliation with the law firm which I had joined in founding, following the years of practicing alone in Harlem, and continued work on some cases, while at the same time making some lecture engagements and working on publishing commitments.

With the transition from city to island, Bengt became our neighbor, how excellent a neighbor both Anthony and I were to appreciate as my health became a crisis in the months following our immigration. That first winter on Block Island was arduous. No accurate and, as it turned out, no competent diagnosis of my ailment had been accomplished, despite resort to various doctors in the city, and none was to be had until a fortnight was spent at Roosevelt Hospital, in the spring of 1968, when it was established that I suffered from a radical impairment in my body's capability to absorb, digest, and utilize food. In the meantime, during the months of winter, there had been a sudden and accelerating loss of weight—nearly sixty pounds in seven weeks—accompanied by a gradual intensification of pain assaulting me intermittently at first, but then become incessant, unremitting, and, as it seemed to me, insatiable. I was dying of malnutrition. I had underway the writing of a paperback book commissioned by the Confraternity of Christian Doctrine, entitled *Imposters of God* (it has since been published), which I dutifully tried to complete; but the pain matured, from an interruption and distraction, into a kind of possession of not only my body but my person, so that the facility of concentration was crippled. There were as well some long-standing commitments for lectures which, I suppose out of some inherited Puritan virtue, I attempted to honor, although Bengt joined Anthony in vehemently opposing these trips as suicidal, which, indeed, they literally were. I fulfilled several in a state of unspeakable distress, but my stoicism became exhausted, and many engagements were canceled under the duress of the pain.

Whatever diversion happened that winter was mediated to me through Anthony and through Bengt. More than that, the burden of living in the same household with me could only have been a solitary and demoralizing one for Anthony had it not been for Bengt's concern for each of us. Bengt is an inspired raconteur and we would often dine with him and talk long into the nights. The conversations were versatile and far-ranging, though in my recollection they had a theological coherence relating quite diverse topics like politics and food and Block Island history and urban existence and corruption of the churches and racial conflict and inflation and medical ethics and poetry and Sweden and war and work and weather. I take for granted that readers of mine realize that theology is dissimilar from both philosophy and religion: theology is not speculative, on one hand, theology is not self-justifying, on the other, and theology is not so eminent as to be aloof from life as it is, as are those two exercises. Theology is concerned with the implication of the Word of God in the world's common life. In this context, it must be recognized and affirmed that every man, *if* he reflects upon the event of his own life in this world, is a theologian. It is only in this sense that I tolerate being sometimes called a theologian myself, though I am aware that I am frequently referred to as a "lay theologian" in an accusatory tone by ecclesiastics and by academic theologians who mean it as a put down and as a way of disavowing my public views. Anyway,

Bengt is a theologian in the sense mentioned
—though it may surprise him to learn that—and
because his reflections are not casual but really
rather rigorous, I believe he is a good theologian.

Thus it was that months and months later—
after that strenuous and somber winter, after
the trip to Roosevelt Hospital, after the failure
of every therapy, after surgery, after returning
to Block Island, in the midst of recuperation—
when Bengt talked of writing about the whole
experience, he spoke with an authority, which
I could not ignore and which my various
qualms did not dismiss.

the health care scandals

Aside from a knowledge within myself, only a few persons apprehended the extremity of my situation. I had kept this from my family until days before the surgery, when I visited my parents and they saw me. My father, I realized, intuited how imminent death was and was able to admit it to himself, though he said little to me; my mother, I think, knew as much but was loathe to admit it, as if by not acknowledging it the truth would change.

How grave the issue was had not been known even after the examinations and tests—which I endured as tortures—at Roosevelt Hospital in the spring of 1968. Hindsight establishes that the diagnosis constructed from these trials was accurate, but incomplete, since the complications which had to be confronted during the surgery were such that could not be detected except in surgical exploration. Recourse to surgery had been closely considered at Roosevelt, but a decision was taken to attempt medical therapy aimed at arresting the drastic weight loss and at mitigating the pain, with the condition that I would return to Block Island under a regime of medication and rest through the spring and summer, and then the matter would be reappraised.

I left Roosevelt Hospital with an optimism, engendered less by how I felt physically than how I felt psychically: at least now I had confidence that I was in the care of doctors who possessed competence and, more importantly, diligence, and whose interest was more medical than commercial.

I had not had reason for any such confidence until then. By the time I entered Roosevelt Hospital, in fact, my morale was something like that of the woman with the hemorrhage, described in the Gospel according to Saint Mark, "who had suffered much under many physicians, and had spent all that she had, and was no better but rather grew worse." It commonly requires a piteous effort to locate a conscientious doctor in the city. To obtain a doctor at all is a notorious problem among the poor, as I had learned secondhand, while living in East Harlem, from the recurrent troubles that my neighbors and clients encountered in seeking medical assistance or hospital care. Lives were—they still are —daily being jeopardized, impaired or, often, lost because of underequipped, overtaxed, understaffed hospital and health facilities and because of the unavailability or absence of sur-

geons, physicians, nurses and other medical
personnel. Allow, on top of this, for the stag-
gering patientload (the numbers of human beings in need of attention would be even
greater) and for haste, misdiagnosis and other
human error, and the conclusion is inescapable
that the public health bureaucracy has not
only failed the poor of this society, but is actually inimical to the health of the poor. That
remains the general situation despite the valiant
spirit of those scarce doctors and hospital professionals who work in places like East Harlem,
both in the municipal hospitals and in private
endeavors such as the clinic established by Dr.
Beatrice Berle at the behest of the East Harlem
Protestant Parish. The persistent scandal concerning care for the health of the poor in the
city should not, however, cause the parallel situation among the bourgeoisie to be overlooked.
Hospital inflation alone—the per diem basic
price for merely occupying space in a hospital
has tripled in the past decade—has placed
health beyond the means of the middle classes,
just as the inability to pay has put health out
of the reach of the poor. For the middle classes
this is only occasionally, and then, only partially, mitigated by gambling on insurance
schemes. In America, hospitalization is a disagreeable luxury, and the significant difference
between the poor and the bourgeoisie is not in
effectual insurance protection for either or in
the capability of the middle classes to afford

25

what the poor cannot buy, but in the facility of
the middle classes in obtaining credit. Accelerating inflation and easy access to expensive
credit—a combination which is active in other
realms of society as well as health—work together to make the purchase price of medical
and hospital care for the middle classes their
indefinite indebtedness. The ethics of class dic-
tate that a contrary public illusion be maintained, but the truth is that in this way, and in
some others, the American bourgeoisie become
empirically more impoverished than the poor.
At that point, the poor may still complain of
their neglected or wasted health, but at least
they retain a certain dignity as human beings,
while the middle classes are consigned to a
ridiculous and far more ignominious poverty.
Compounding the irony, of course, is the fact
that even the gross indebtedness, which the
middle classes incur to secure what health care
they receive, is subsidized heavily by the poor.
I refer to the wage scales still prevalent among
non-professional hospital employees—orderlies,
kitchen help, maintenance personnel and the
like—recruited largely from among the urban
poor, especially blacks and Puerto Ricans. A
few years ago I was among those instrumental
in the passage of legislation in New York that
insured collective bargaining rights for these
employees and the recognition of Local 1199
of the Hospital and Drug Employees Union—
one of the few uncorrupted labor unions sur-

viving in this land. That gave me some insight into how so-called volunteer hospitals operated by churches or charitable corporations sought to compensate for high costs by paying wages that often amounted to much less than the person employed might receive by applying for welfare assistance. In that manner, the frightfully meager wages of hospital workers paid for part of the patients' expense. Since that time, there has been an improvement in New York on this score, and an effort has been made to seek similar fairness for hospital workers in other places, notably Charleston, South Carolina, but, for the most part, this form of the poor subsidizing the hospitalization of the other classes continues.

In addition to the price of health, the bourgeoisie share with the poor a problem of accessibility to doctors and specialists. Yet, where the matter for the poor is usually one of an absence or shortage of needed and appropriate practitioners, rather than the conscientiousness of those few who are available, the question for the middle classes is the trustworthiness of the medical profession. I do not have in mind what quacks or charlatans there may be on the scene, the self-interest of the profession polices them somewhat. I mean, instead, the dilettantes of medicine who forswear their own competence and imitate the volume principle of other businesses to maximize profit by the high turnover of patients. Their speciality is glib diagnosis and the indulgence of the sick with the condiments of medical care—useless prescriptions, unnecessary procedures, frivolous referrals to asserted consultants. Thus many patients are importuned into needlessly becoming repeat and, sometimes, dependent customers. They are the medical entrepreneurs who intend to take all that the traffic will bear and, as in some other enterprises, high fees, bearing no significant positive relationship to the service marketed, are a deliberate public relations representation in substitution for capable performance. It seems dubious to me that such ethics —which, shrewdly practiced, are quite safe from condemnation as malpractice—in any profession, occupation or business, though they be popular in most all pursuits in this society, can be countenanced; be that as it may, their prevalence in the medical arts is poignantly reprehensible as a literal trafficking in human suffering. It is, after all, one thing not to get your money's worth in some transaction involving goods, it becomes another matter where the transaction directly risks your health. Such parasitical physicians are concentrated heavily in the city because of the enormous backlog of potential patients there and because of the relative safety from scrutiny in the city as compared with a smaller community in which every doctor is a public figure. And it is the middle classes, with their ready credit, more or less reduced to shopping for a doctor in the yellow pages, who are the convenient prey.

No reader, at this juncture, will suffer surprise at learning that prior to my entry into Roosevelt Hospital, I had been a victim of just such a predator doctor. I do not, by mentioning him, discount my own procrastination in seeking medical help, although I think I do not rationalize that by saying that the very difficulty in locating a trustworthy physician prolonged my malingering somewhat. In any case, impelled by acute distress I went to one doctor who had attended me three years earlier during what was then said to be a passing gastric ailment. His treatment at that time consisted of his requiring that I spend some days resting, with mild sedation, while being fed intravenously, in a private hospital in which he was an investor as well as a staff member. I retained some suspicions about that episode: I could not figure out, for sure, whether I had been conned or cured or both. This doctor was familiar with my medical history, including the records I had secured for him about gall bladder surgery I had undergone at the Peter Bent Brigham Hospital in Boston during my final year as a student at the Harvard Law School, or, at the least, he already had access to the relevant data, and that had some weight in favor of recourse to him. Soon enough, the pain exceeded my misgivings and I took the line of least resistance and did go to him. Four months, a thousand

innocuous pills, a score of redundant X rays, repeated office consultations, and a prolific ac-
cumulation of bills later, common sense, and,
one might say, an instinct for survival, transcended the pain and my suspicions returned
militantly. When I resorted to this practitioner,
the pain, still intermittent, seemed to be located
in the back, somewhat below and in between
the shoulder blades, toward the left side. While
in his charge, the pain had so intensified that I
had difficulty walking without assistance, and
I could no longer either stand or be seated
without enervation. Meanwhile, the sudden,
rapid and drastic loss of weight was happening. The doctor's view—I withhold the term
diagnosis—was that I suffered a muscular dis-
order in the back; his remedies were literally
superficial—massages, saunas, liniments, and
frequent hot baths, plus those innocuous pills.
Urinalysis showing a sugar problem prompted
him to prescribe orinase and to inquire whether
either of my parents was diabetic, but did not
inspire him to make further investigation as to
my metabolism. That this physician's conscience for his patients was less than alert im-
pressed me decisively one morning when he
proposed, enthusiastically, as it seemed to me
at the time, to fit me with a back brace, pur-
suant to his muscular theory and persistent in
ignoring the evidences of a metabolic rather
than muscular difficulty. *That will cripple me*,
I thought. A brace would invalid me indefi-

nitely and, incidentally, make me a perpetual patient. I nodded toward the scales in the examination room where we were talking. They indicated that since my last visit to his parlors, less than a month's time, I had lost more than forty pounds. "The last thing in the world I need is a girdle!" I told him, and turned, and left.

This experience of mine is not, as far as I observe, unusual, but rather typical of the problems with which middle-class folk have to contend in obtaining access to competent health care, particularly in the city. Coupled with encumbrances of medical and hospital inflation, the lot of the bourgeoisie in this society, so far as health is concerned, is no safer or no better in any other significant way than is that of the poor. By that token, reform in medical and hospital financing and improvement in the distribution of medical and hospital services cannot seriously be envisioned unless both the poor and the middle classes comprehend how they are each being sacrificed, and until both realize the compatibility of their respective self-interests and are thus enabled to act together.

The most basic issue is, manifestly, that health has become *primarily* a commercial enterprise in this land, which even the mythology of Dr. Gillespie cannot conceal. There is ample documentation of the subversion of human health by the commercialization of the medical profession and its satellite disciplines, occupations and industries. That is to be found not only in the frequency of occurrences, such as my own experience just recited, nor merely in the broader context, which has been mentioned, of the problems of availability and accessibility for both poor and middle classes or of the fact that, generally, neither poor nor bourgeois people can actually afford the health care they need when they need it. Much more can be cited: the gross abuse of medicare and medicaid through fraudulent collection of fees for services never rendered and, sometimes, for fictitious patients; the similar, familiar, if more discreet, padding practices that have become virtually customary by doctors and hospitals where private insurance schemes are applicable; the inversion of priorities in medical research occasioned by the profit motive; the vain emphasis often given to cosmetic, as distinguished from organic, procedures in surgery; the diverting of private monies given for health purposes to the maintenance of the health-charities bureaucracy with its elaborately wasteful promotional and fund-raising apparatus; the scandals, exposed partially through Senate inquiries, in prescribing, labeling, pricing and marketing drugs and pharmaceuticals; the commercial indoctrination of both the sick and the well to purchase and use potents, tonics, pills, symptomatic remedies and assorted pseudomedicines, frequently abetted by specious professional endorsements. The health business, in its various branches, is one in which a primitive *laissez-faire* ethic still dominates with all the comparable cruel and savage consequences for human life that the same ethic . has fostered in other realms where it has been allowed without bridle, and, lately, this process has been accentuated by the attempts, substantially successful, of the American Medical Association to politicize the doctors, in order to enhance their commercial advantages.

This is, admittedly, a victim's diatribe which omits compliments, which some physicians and surgeons deserve, and does not mention the generosity of some hospitals or the selflessness of many hospital personnel of all sorts or the dedicated imagination of many in research or the honesty and viable conscience of others in the health industry. I do not ignore any of these. In fact, I bear unqualified gratitude and admiration for those who took care of me at Roosevelt Hospital, as I have already said, and, later, at the Columbia-Presbyterian Hospital, as well as Bernard Abramson, the doctor of Block Island. Yet it does not honor that esteem to gainsay or to minimize the corruption, which the commercialization of health care in America has wrought. Moreover, I can complain as I have about the doctors and their associates because, as a lawyer, I am mindful that my own profession is about equally vulnerable to analogous indictment. The devotion of the legal profession, for generations, to com-

mercial interests, at the expense of service to
the remainder of the community and, especially, to the profound deprivation of the poor
in their legal rights and causes has become, by
now, notorious, and has been significantly responsible for bringing this nation to the brink
of insurrection and a totalitarian repression.
The intent of my own practice as a lawyer has
been to oppose that. It is by this same authority,
in the context of what I learned in illness and
what I observed as a patient, that I can protest,
without arrogance, I trust, the precedence
which greed has gained over health in American society.

therapy and theology

Through the spring and summer of 1968, following my release from Roosevelt Hospital, I remained on Block Island pursuing the regime of rest and medicine which, it was hoped, would arrest the weight loss and alleviate the pain. Massive quantities of animal enzymes, taken with small portions of food every two or three hours, were tried to remedy the former; various drugs were prescribed from time to time for the latter. It was arranged that I would return to the city periodically to be examined and for follow-up tests at the hospital, as might be indicated, and, while on the Island, remain under the general care and surveillance of the doctor there.

I was loyal to the new way of life, and within a month of leaving Roosevelt there had been a perceptible, if ever so modest, improvement: I gained a pound. For a while, too, I enjoyed spasmodic relief from pain, at least just after taking a prescription for that purpose. These evident gains soon faded. By summer's end I weighed the proverbial ninety-nine pounds; a succession of increasingly potent pain antidotes proved helpful only briefly, as my tolerance for such material matured and as the severity and continuity of the pain grew. Much reluctance on my part to confess it would not mitigate the truth of that season: the therapy was failing.

To have rest was the hard aspect of the therapy, if only because of its novelty for me. For a dozen years, since being graduated from law school, the pace of my life had been hectic and crowded. Though the time I lived and practiced law in Harlem had been lonely—and thus exacting in a psychical sense—it had also been arduous enough physically and intellectually so that I was not self-conscious about that. Subsequently, when two colleagues from Harvard Law School, Frank Patton and William S. Ellis, joined with me in founding a law firm, which both inherited the Harlem practice and diversified with other cases, I undertook the keeping of regular and more conventional office hours. At about the same period, I began to write and publish and, in turn, receive many invitations for lecture engagements and preaching assignments. These responsibilities meant that after spending a day in court or at the firm, I would devote three or four hours at night to writing, and then on weekends be on the road for speaking engagements. There were, at this same time, frequent journeys overseas, sometimes

as a member of the Faith and Order Commission of the World Council of Churches, on other
occasions for lecture tours, or, as with a trip
to Vietnam in 1966 that converted me to radical opposition to the American war there, to
observe, to listen, and, hopefully, to learn. The
household which Anthony and I had established in Manhattan was an hospitable one, and
he and I shared there in an unpretentious—
and almost unintentional—pastoral ministry to
an astonishing diversity and far-flung number
of persons. Besides all that, we each dabbled
in city politics, tenants' strikes, assorted demon-
strations and protests, and the affairs of a congregation. Occasionally, through all of this activity, there would be episodes for me of
devastating fatigue, and, then, spasms of pain,
like the one, mentioned earlier, by which I was
misfortuned to become acquainted with that
dilettante physician and was briefly hospital-
ized.

On the whole, however, I thrived upon the
tension in which I labored—or so it seems to me
—though I did recognize, vaguely, an improvi-
dence of such an existence. If I procrastinated
in the face of lucid warnings within my own
body of disease at work and failed, until entering Roosevelt, to locate competent medical
care, I also sought no help, such as it might
have been, from psychiatry, despite now and
then considering the matter. In retrospect, I
have a small regret that I did not explore this

possibility. I did not do so, I suppose, because of an inherited Yankee attitude which begins with a general skepticism toward the field, on a practical level, and ends with a suspicion that resort to a psychiatrist can easily if not inevitably be an exercise of extravagant vanity. On the other hand, I was not inhibited from consuming much alcohol during these busy years in legal practice and on the lecture circuit and whatnot. Consistent with my denominational identity as an Episcopalian, I had, as an adult, always had an enthusiasm for drinking, but, as my days became more feverish, I knew that I was becoming unduly dependent upon alcohol. It was no longer a condiment of living, but a substitute, though scarcely a sensible one, for rest and, sometimes, for food, and, as might be expected, an insulation from the incessancy of daily demands. And, as sporadic pain visited me, I sometimes used alcohol for a superficial and transient relief it seemed to bring. I stopped drinking completely in January of 1968. It was no New Year's resolution; it involved no exertion of willpower, no positive thinking, no prayer—at least in any conventional connotation, no admonitions from doctors, no inspiration from friends. I just stopped because I had lost a taste for alcohol. It was, as far as I can discern, a physiological happening: my body would no longer tolerate the stuff.

Meanwhile, I had taken some initiative to alter the pace of things. I decided to take leave

of daily practice, curtail public engagements,
and spend a year or more reading and thinking
and writing. I had had a notion for quite a
while about a work in moral theology, specifically, so to speak, in *American* moral theology
—seeking to relate the American experience of
society and nationhood to the biblical saga and
social witness. This is a pitifully neglected
realm. There has been curiously little moral
theology, which has had currency and impact
in this country in the present century, that can
be said to have indigenous American origina-
tion. Most moral theology which has been ar-
ticulated in the American context has actually
been composed out of European experience
and transplanted here. Aside from fugitive materials, the singular exception in this situation
has been the immensely influential and useful
contributions of Reinhold Niebuhr in the era
between the Great Depression and the end of
the Second World War. Neither the moral theology imported, as it were, from Europe nor the
witness of Niebuhr is vitiated by the fact, but
it does remain an odd void that a moral theology related to the distinctive American experience since the detonation of the first atomic
weapon or since America became a pervasive
imperial presence in the world or since technology and race became uniquely juxtaposed in
social crisis in America has not yet emerged.
All things considered, it seemed to me the time
to pursue that. I received a Guggenheim Fel-

lowship for this sabbatical, altered my relationship with Ellis, Stringfellow & Patton from partner to counsel to the firm, and prepared to embark on the project, living on Block Island but planning one excursion to Eastern Europe and to Cambridge University, as well as some domestic travels along the way. I made a modest headway on this agenda, despite increasingly frequent interruptions of pain, until, in the spring of 1968, the illness had become virtually immobilizing and I entered upon the therapy determined by the diagnosis accomplished at Roosevelt Hospital.

I have not had an explicit conviction about where my interest about what I call an American moral theology might lead. Conceivably, the void I sense has not been filled because it cannot be. Perhaps the void is in itself *the* significant insight into the American national experience of the last quarter century, so far as moral theology is concerned. Whatever the case, this represents an issue to which I mean to return and a work I want, somehow, to finish. In fact I feel little frustration about it, since I have never abandoned or even postponed it in my mind, and since the experience of my disease appears to me, ironically, relevant to the subject. It could hardly be otherwise for me because, insofar as I may be said to be a theologian, I am not a theological scholar (I have not the temperament for that) but an empirical theologian (which the scholar is also, if in a less obvious manner, whether it is admitted or not). Meager jokes had passed between Anthony and me during these months of sickness and convalescence as to whether the pain would affect my theology; obviously it has, both in ways which I can discern and in ways of which I can never be completely aware. That is exactly as it should be. Or, to put it a bit differently, Christians are Hebrews in their mentality, not Greeks. Biblical theology, especially the moral theology of the Bible, is itself empirical, a testimony wrought in experience, not academic, in the sense of abstraction. There is nothing whatever in the experience in history of men or nations that is not essentially theological, and the discipline of academics is not to speculate or innovate from some (supposed) stance on the outside of common experience but to expound and enlighten empirical reality, relating inheritance, memory and the happenings of the past to the contemporary scene, alert for portents of that which is to come in this world. In the biblical witness, the Incarnation is the illustrious instance in point: the event of God acting in history in Jesus Christ addresses the experience of men contemporaneously. That is the case, according to Saint Paul, *even* where and when human beings have never heard explicitly of Jesus Christ. There is no "once upon a time," much less hypothetical, connotation attaching to the Incarnation, and, thus, to affirm the Incarnation is not a matter of having a blessed memory, much less of earnest persuasion, but to suffer this action of God empirically, here and now.

This is why those preachers from the churches who treat biblical material as normative in furnishing rules of conduct and penalty are actually involved in a denial of the most elementary word of the Bible. It is also why the whole emphasis in so-called Christian education in the mainline denominations to "make the Gospel relevant" to modern man conceals a dreadful hang-up which abuses the character of the biblical word. The former (obviously Billy Graham is the archetype of these preachers) regard God as a threatening, arbitrary, fearsome figure imprisoned in an ancient era, of which the Bible tells, without contemporary vitality yet still requiring a simplistic, mechanical conformity from human beings nowadays. This is, truly, a view of God as dead, save for what vindication there is in memory; it pictures God exacting tribute from the grave. The other case (the Methodist Publishing House—a skillful equivocator on the issue of race, by the way—takes huge profits from marketing such curriculum materials in congregations) also assumes that God was only empirically active a very long time ago, but that now editors have to elaborately transpose the biblical saga in order to make sense of it in terms of present circumstances. This approach holds that God is an absentee from the modern scene; it envisions God as alive but truant. It is hard to decide which of these perversions is the more scandalous.

However that may be, the Gospel esteems God in a more excellent way than either erstwhile preachers or curriculum makers. The biblical witness *is* normative, but not legislatively; it is normative in the sense that the Bible is the exemplary story of God's consistent, militant, continuing and patient involvement in the history of mankind. The biblical affirmation beholds the specific events of biblical times as characteristic of God's vocation for all men, in all times and places, prior to the biblical era and ever since and evermore. It is this same surrogate, representative, characteristic, exemplary, "normative"—if you wish—significance of the Bible that designates the holy. This is what holiness means. The biblical saga is, thus, the holy history of the world. And the problem of "relevance" between the holy history and our history is obviated because, by its very exemplary character, *the holy history is,* as it were, *concurrent with contemporary history.*

Whatever discoveries, whatever data, whatever insight theological scholarship offers (and whatever scholarship does offer is to be welcomed as a gift) must never be merely pedantic, but must always be disciplined and, indeed, authenticated empirically. It is the empirical realm which is the constant environment of the biblical witness—of the *living* Word of God.

43

the ambiguity of pain

The therapy failed and I became possessed by pain.

There is an ambiguity in pain which is truly exquisite. It is no wonder that medical science is so ignorant about what pain is, beyond knowing what any victim of pain realizes without asking a doctor: pain involves a delicate joinder of the physiological and the psychosomatic and is *never* but one or the other of these. Nor, given the dignity of the mystery of pain, is it very surprising that so little has been uttered, since Job himself, concerning the theology of pain. American religiosity (as distinguished from biblical faith or theology), meanwhile, remains so hapless and absurd that, generally, it denies the reality of pain or else treats pain as a punishment for immorality. It is such religiose attitudes about pain that explain the profound, and primitive, indifference of institutional religion in America to human suffering occasioned by social injustice. Moreover, by the way, the association of these typical views of

pain with the equally entrenched notion that
acquisition or control of money or credit is an
evidence of virtue is what has allowed the commercialization of medicine, of which previous
complaint has been made. Obviously, to the religious, if pain is either an illusion or a punishment and if money or its equivalent signifies
moral rectitude, then one must be able to purchase the absence of or relief from pain, and
those who cannot do so have only themselves
to blame for their plight.

Part of the ambiguity attending pain is at-
tributable to ignorance and some of it to prejudice, but much of that ambiguity has to do
with the sentimentalization of pain in the experience of a particular person. I found that
so myself. To maintain lucidity in the midst
of pain requires an effort at once enormous and
resourceful. In pain, as much or more than
physical health, sanity itself is always at issue.
The issue is present, subtly, even where pain is
minimal and transient; it is there blatantly
where pain is ferocious and obstinate. In the
latter circumstances, the temptation of delusion and, beyond that, the danger of hallucination have no ruth. Moreover, the ambiguity of
pain, specifically as related to lucidity, is accentuated by time, a matter about which something more is to be said in another chapter, so
let it be here recognized that I am actually
writing now about my memory of pain—not

only the memory of pain in my mind, but the memory of pain in my body—as distinct from my pain. In doing so, there is an element of distortion between the experience and the memory, though I can do nothing about that, except acknowledge it.

I said that the ambiguity of pain is exquisite: pain is inexhaustibly ambiguous. It is, I learned, difficult to identify pain, unless by its apparent absence. In the early days of my disease when the pain was episodic, it seemed to me that I could distinguish what pain is, but whatever facility of discrimination I then, or before then, had, I lost as the illness deepened and the pain became relentless and, paradoxically, so familiar that I ceased to think of myself as in pain. I am not talking about bearing pain with a stiff upper lip, or any kind of stoicism, I am referring to a state of the person, body and mind, which becomes so vulnerable to pain that there remains no comprehension of what freedom from pain is. I remember that.

While en route to this extremity, I had sought respite in various diversions. The aim in such exercises is to find a distraction sufficient to, temporarily, displace the pain as a fascination. It is, I suppose, a form of delusive sublimation. But as my immunity to medical painkillers, as they are somewhat euphemistically called, grew stronger, I resorted to such devices. I persevered in trying to work—to finish the much postponed *Imposters of God* manuscript, to further the

Guggenheim project, to deal with the mail. The
output was arduous, the yield meager and indifferent. More helpful, for a while, was work
involving (for me) greater, but briefer, concentration combined with manual effort: I learned
how to make bread. At dawn, on many morn-
ings, I left a sleepless bed and did that. I hesitate
to mention it here, though it was a prominent,
sometimes the only, event of some of those days,
apart from the pain, because there is an odd
romanticism in this culture associated with
homemade bread, notably among urbanite
snobs, hippies, and advocates of liturgical renewal. Though I have some involvement with
all three of these factions in society, I think
there was nothing corny, nothing grandiose,
and nothing specially symbolic about my bread.
The fact is my body's assimilation of food had
become so harmed by this juncture that I was
hungry all the time, which furnished a simple
incentive for baking bread that other chores
within the capabilities I then retained did not
have. Television, which I suspect was invented
as a distraction, proved of little avail against
pain and may well have aggravated it. I had
not been habituated to watching the machine,
aside from state funerals, Senate hearings and
the like, and, only half-facetiously, I thought
that, when a set is on, it is actually television
that is watching you. So on days and nights
when, it seemed, I was consigned to do no more
than linger in distress, I and it watched each

other. I will, here, spare the world the obvious
diatribe concerning contrivance, redundancy
and inanity. Nor will I boast about my experi-
ments to improve the medium by keeping the
picture, but turning off the sound and compos-
ing one's own plot to accompany what could be
seen (the reverse experiment, imagining scenes
to go with the sound, is also an improvement).
What greatly bothered me about television—
and, thus, did provide some diversion—was its
saturation with religious propaganda of the
most indulgent sort. I refer to programs—
"Gentle Ben," "Green Acres," "Leave It To
Beaver," for a few examples—which project an
image of the good society as a lily-white, Anglo-
Saxon, Protestant, pastoral life governed by self-
evident verities in which simplistic virtue
abounds, generally embodied in a policeman.
The presupposition of such shows is straight out
of nineteenth-century, rural, white denominationalism and, whatever apologetic there might
have been for this in the last century, there is
none tenable in this century in the midst of
cybernetics, urbanization, racial conflict and the
militarization of the police. Meanwhile, there
has never been any serious warrant biblically
for such a view, as has been noted in another
context. That this peculiar sectarianism, implicitly racist, grossly paternalistic, intolerant toward any non-conformity flourishes, and fills so
much television time, cultivates neither verity
nor virtue; it in truth nurtures and exploits the

49

spirit of vengeance and repression among the white majority whose guilt about race and poverty and the city is anyway so pathological that they are defenseless against such manipulation. To this extent, I found recourse to television edifying. I had known how operative the backlash psychology had become in politics, what with Mr. Nixon's "forgotten Americans," and George Wallace's populism, Sam Yorty's incitements, and the phenomenon of Mario Proccaccino, but I had not realized how that same destructive sentiment was being inculcated hour after hour, day after day by the folks of "Mayberry R.F.D."

Reading proved more effective in providing diverting intervals from the pain. My span of concentration became too brief to read a book, though more than adequate for the Providence *Journal*. The New York *Times*, on Sunday, was just too formidable. The two things to which I most often turned to read, for my purpose, were the Psalter and the Sears, Roebuck and Company catalog. I had not previously had occasion to do more than scan either, though I had frequently been in circumstances where each would be cited as authority. Now I found comfort in both. They are remarkably similar volumes. With their marvelous diversity, a man with a little diligence can shop through their pages virtually certain of locating something to suit a desire or need or other disposition of the moment. I recalled, as one might anticipate, the famed remark of Karl Barth about a Christian being a man who has the Bible in one hand and the day's newspaper in the other, simultaneously attentive to the Word and the world. The Psalms, with their terrible esteem for the godliness of God, and Sears, with its infinite attention to the creatureliness of human beings and its nice detail of American culture, make apt companions for the Christian as a common reader.

One after another, such comforts or distractions as I knew were neutralized by pain. The issue drawn was whether to numbly await the perfection of pain in death or whether, somehow, pain would be transcended. Yet that concealed another issue: the vanity which pain instills in its victims. It is the vanity implicated in pain, more than the hurt itself, which has to be transcended if a victim is to remain a human being, whether or not the pain eventuates as death.

When I speak of the vanity engendered by pain, I intend a larger meaning than the facility of pain to attract attention to those who suffer it and something distinguishable from sentiments of self-pity which the afflicted may indulge. These are the more superficial vanities of pain. On the other hand, I do not particularly have in mind human beings in such poignant circumstances that aberrations of the vanity implicit in pain occur, as seems to be the situation in both sadism and masochism. What I do mean is that peculiar vanity in which justification (or the moral significance of a person's existence) is attributed to the visitation and endurance of pain, whether such an attribution is made by the victim or those who are nearby witnesses or by society at large.

As befits a monasterial style of life, I suppose, my experience of pain was seldom mentioned in conversation in the Block Island household, though, now and then, in excruciation, I would utter the name of Jesus, not as a common profanity, but as a curse upon the pain and, really, as a curse upon the power of death. Beyond that, it did not need to be talked about; it was a pervasive, totalitarian presence, a foreigner to life in our midst which could not be ignored and which words would not diminish, yet which, paradoxically, words might intensify.

The putative interdependence of pain and justification harks back, of course, to the barbaric Protestant idea that pain is punishment for immorality, a penalty to be paid for displeasing the Almighty, an inverse way of obtaining justification by works where bearing pain is substituted for doing good deeds. The pursuit of justification by *any* means—moralistic conduct, dogmatic conformity, charitable enterprise, daily work, or burnt offerings—is, in the biblical perspective, the essence of human vanity in its denial of God's freedom to affirm life without contingency, dependency or equivocation. Such notions of justification refute God's capability of love, and to view pain as a means of justification—even for the most apparently reprehensible person—is an especially pathetic ridicule of God as well as a radical demeaning of the human vocation. It ends in futility—as all practice of justification by works does—in a bizarre futility in which the victim becomes an idolator of his own pain.

Pain, manifestly, is not, however, the ultimate idol, but only a demigod representing death. The same is true of other varieties of works, but with pain, as contrasted with charities or rituals or pietism or whatnot, surrogation to the power of death is the more obvious since pain is literally a symptom of the advent of death. To endure pain is to suffer anticipation of death, in both mind and body. The experience of pain is a foretaste of the event of death. Pain is an ambassador of death. Pain is one of death's disguises, though not one of the more subtle ones. It is the surrogate, really, servant relationship evident between pain and death which causes me to write of pain so much in personified terms. Death, after all, is no abstract idea, nor merely a destination in time, nor just an occasional happening, nor only a reality for human beings, but, both biblically and empirically, death names a moral power claiming sovereignty over all men and all things in history. Apart from God Himself, death is a *living* power greater—because death survives them all—than any other moral power in this world of what-

53

ever sort: human beings, nations, corporations, cultures, wealth, knowledge, fame or memory, language, the arts, race, religion. One speaks, therefore, appropriately, and most precisely, of the power of death militant in history after the same manner in which one refers to other moral powers or, indeed, after the manner in which one makes mention of God. And, then, since pain partakes of the reality of death, it is meet as well as accurate to think of pain personified: to regard pain as an acolyte of the power of death.

a false work ethic

That a view of pain as justifying is theologically corrupt, and, more importantly, is morally corrupting to a victim of pain does not exhaust the theological significance of pain. In the course of my illness, while the pain grew more and more intense and enervating, physically and psychically, it became morally more debilitating, as it extended its claim for my attention and enlarged its prominence in all my relationships. Pain threatened to become both occupation and preoccupation. By the time that I was no longer able to work in any ordinary sense and was seeking small diversions in the Sears catalog or by baking bread, I began to realize that, in truth, *pain had become my work*. The resemblance of pain to work, in my circumstances, was startling: pain commandeered, engaged and exhausted all my faculties, energies and talents; pain tested all my weaknesses and shortcomings; pain filled most of the time and dictated the use of all of the time—a day would be organized, insofar as it had any organization, according to the periods pre-empted in pain; what relief or rest there was constituted a preparedness for pain still to come and to be coped with; pain elicited recognition, and even admiration, from others; pain tempted me to vainly suppose it justified my very being. Whatever else might be said about the reality of pain, it bears virtually every attribute of the experience of work.

Americans are heirs to a mythology of work which remains rhetorically potent in pulpits, political compaigns, and civic rituals, though in practice it has long since been dishonored or abandoned by exactly those Americans most fond of its recitation. The central notion is that work is good—a good for society since work is a deterrent to anti-social behavior and a good for society in terms of that which work produces and distributes, and, then, a good for the worker both in the satisfaction alleged to inhere in the effort itself and in the rewards which accrue from work. In more elaborate version, the myth fixes upon the products and/or the rewards of work to assign virtue—literally, as with pain, *justification*—to the worker. The primitive American work ethic has been that a man is morally worthy, and entitled to compensation, where his labor is tangibly productive.

This inherited idea of work is attended these days by absurd illusions and gross hypocrisy, whatever may have been its integrity in the eighteenth and nineteenth centuries. For one thing, work as a restraint to protest, rebellion, or even crime can only be esteemed as a good for society by those who wield power in the established institutions; to those dispossessed of power, work is at least an intimidation and at worst an enslavement. And, one notices, that this same notion of work as a social good because it is a deterrent to behavior condemned by the-powers-that-be has, paradoxically, been made for maintaining fixed levels of unemployment. This is a significant paradox because it points to the fact that the theological relationships between men and the rest of creation, evident in the various forms of non-work—unemployment, unemployability, leisure, play, retirement—are quite the same as in work.

Meanwhile, the view of work as morally justifying and deserving of reward where tangibly productive began to be undermined with the primary mechanization of agriculture and the advent of the Industrial Revolution more than a century ago. By the middle of the present century in this country, technology together with radical changes in the conception of wealth have rendered this ethic both obsolete and corny, so far as the employed white bourgeoisie are concerned since a majority of these Americans are now engaged in jobs which have no moral standing as defined by the classical work ethic. The old notion that the social usefulness for human life of tangible products somehow made the worker who produced the goods morally

57

worthy is not only inapplicable where there are no goods produced, it is equally inappropriate where products are redundant luxuries, or where the market for products is promotionally engineered and manipulated or where in fact it is the package rather than the product which is marketed. That the inherited Protestant work ethic no longer fits the facts of white-bourgeois employment substantially explains a shift in emphasis from products of work to rewards of work as a basis of attributing virtue to the worker. Among the middle-class whites, what a man receives as compensation (or, more recently, the extent of his access to credit) rather than what a man does, or the character of his intangible work or "services," is computed as his moral worth. While technology made such a shift more or less inevitable, it might nonetheless have wrought a defensible amendment to the old ethic if more conscientious attention were given to the ethics of compensation. In reality, however, it seems to matter little how a man gains control of wealth or acquires credit—by inheritance, investment, theft, luck or labor—in imputing a justified status to him.

This discrepancy between ethic and practice for the employed white bourgeoisie, accentuated though it be by rhetorical prominence in the white subculture, might still be regarded as an innocuous hypocrisy were it not for the vehemence with which the obsolete idea of tangible work as justifying is enforced, with a literal vengeance, against the poor in general and the non-white poor in particular. That the poor should be obliged to do some visible work —raking the leaves in the city parks or the like —as a condition for receiving welfare supplements has now been raised to the dignity of national policy. (The presidential address enunciating this was in substance a sermon on the Protestant work ethic.) The moral absurdity of the Nixon-Moynahan welfare "reform" is, of course, that the same technological change that has so drastically curtailed tangibly productive work for the prosperous classes has also largely eliminated the necessity of such jobs for the poor. In consequence, the poor, if they are to be employed at all, must either be sufficiently trained for the same kinds of non-productive jobs that the middle classes occupy or else activities in which the poor already engage (including housework, the rearing of children) or which they could readily undertake if allowed to do so (including study, community organization) must be recognized as work and compensated as such, or, preferably, both of these must be done. The existing welfare policy, and the tortured mentality which informs it, consigns the poor—at best—to an indeterminate status as servants, menial dependents of the middle-class majority. Behind all this, of course, is the implication of the old work ethic that if the products or, now, the rewards of work are the secret of justification for a person, then to be

unemployed or uncompensated indicates moral
defect. And if, thus, by definition of public
policy—not just a harmless or foolish rhetoric—
to be poor is to be a sinner, then to be affluent
must prove moral innocence.

pain as work

What has long troubled me—beyond the pathetic fantasies which the white middle classes entertain about work for extolling themselves while victimizing the poor, both economically and psychologically—is that the inherited work ethic in this society has not, and has never had, any biblical sanction whatever. That it may be called "the Protestant work ethic" refers only to its cultural origins in white, Anglo-Saxon Protestant denominationalism in America, generically a secular phenomenon, and not to any credence the ethic has in the biblical witness.

Biblically, work has to do with the relationships between men and the rest of creation. Embraced in the term is not only the stereotype of man and the soil, but also a fabulous array of other images, to which lucid reference is made in the Bible, of men and the full diversity of the rest of creation: man and the earth, yes; man and nature, to be sure; but, as well, man and all other creatures; man and the ideologies; man and the institutions; man and the corporate entities; man and the environment; man and science; man and technological process; man and the State; man and the family; man and each and every principality or power.

Work, as a biblical word, both designates and characterizes these multiple and simultaneous relationships, or, to be more precise about it, work describes the *broken* relationships between men and the rest of creation, in its remarkable diversity, familiar to every man in this history. Work is a reality of fallen existence, that is, of the present era in which, by the veracity of human experience, all relationships are sundered, all persons and principalities exist in profound disorientation with respect to themselves, their identities and functions, and to one another, and all things are subjected to death, and all experience is premonitive of death. To put it in the Genesis language (without implying anything about the status of the Genesis story as such), work represents the lost dominion of men over the rest of creation. The images of man as Lord of the whole of creation, whose life is sustained by the earth's yield, served by the principalities and enhanced by the other creatures, are, in the common history of mankind—which is to say, in the Fall—inverted: now man is not a sovereign, but a slave; not master but victim; not engaged in the celebration of life, but in working to death. Thus, biblically, work is associated with burden, conflict, aliena-

tion, struggle, sweat, redundant effort, bondage
to time, subsistence, fatigue, drudgery, waste,
futility, the imminence of death. Such is not
only the biblical description of work, but also
the empirical reality of work—plainly and literally so for all the overwhelming masses of humanity that have ever been born. One does not
have to recall ancient feudalisms to discern that,
one has only to behold the contemporary feudalisms in Haiti or Rhodesia; neither does one
have to recall chattel slavery in Rome or in
North America, nor dwell upon child labor or
migrant workers or Siberian exiles or soldiers in
any war in order to document the broken relationship which work is in ordinary experience,
as much as in biblical characterization, because,
for that, one can as well look at the equally hu-
miliated Long Island commuter who works in
order to service his indebtedness, or the absurdity of the Japanese stockbroker who must work
in a gas mask because the industrial expansion
in which he invests has so spoiled the environment, or the deadening conformities that imprison the executives of any corporate bureaucracy.

As the term is here being used, work means
more than a job. It encompasses the entire,
tangled fabric of relationships—or of distorted
or broken relationships—between men and the
rest of creation, including all forms of non-work,
alluded to earlier, such as retirement, play or
other leisure pursuits, unemployment and un-

employability, study or other tasks preliminary to employment. The estrangement and enslavement familiar to men in work remain the essential elements in all of these varieties of non-work and, in American society, the only significant factor which distinguishes work from non-work is the payment of compensation. It is an arbitrary matter—determined by custom, age, race, sex, heredity, organization, promotion, convenience, rather than any intrinsic characteristic of the activity itself, and rather than any inherent merit morally in the activity —what is deemed entitled to compensation. If in some earlier day, social utility provided a test for that, it is no longer applied with either consistency or equity, and, if it should be, as has been mentioned, about half of the white bourgeoisie would lose their compensation, while multitudes of the poor would have to be compensated for effort in which they have been and are now engaged.

I had come to such an understanding of work from both my personal Bible study and my own experience in work, especially during the years in Harlem, and it had long since become the case that I could not differentiate, in my daily existence, between work and non-work. It had seemed to me that I was always at work or that I was never working (whichever way one might state it, it means exactly the same thing), so similar did the essential issues in either work or non-work, as they are nominally called, appear to me to be. In my private experience, whatever the appearances might have been to others, it made no serious difference whether I was in court pleading a case, or on the streets of Harlem, or conferring with a client, or writing at my desk, or in a television interview, or on the lecture circuit, or with other people, or alone, or awake, or asleep. And that I received compensation for some of these, but not for others, was of only incidental consequence and did not alter the character of my own relationship with the rest of creation.

All that came to focus in my illness and helps explain why I came to realize in the months immediately prior to the surgery that the pain I bore had, in truth, become my work, in quite the same sense that my law practice or writing or household chores would be considered work.

My work was my pain: my pain was my work. All work—including all so-called non-work—is pain because work manifests the fallenness between men and the rest of creation, and, since pain is a specific instance and endurance of that same fallenness, pain is work.

This dialectic of pain and work is no mere esoteric theological proposition. It bears most concretely upon the possibility of the transcendence of pain—both the vanity of pain, of which something has already been said, and the pain *per se*. The secret of that transcendence is the same for pain as it is for any other sort of work.

The American mythology concerning work

supposes that the fallenness, or consignment to death, which work embodies can be met and mastered by a man's exercise of choice in the work in which he engages. He must seek and choose some work which fulfills his talents and energies or which is so satisfying in its efforts or rewards as to be accounted the equivalent of self-fulfillment. The matter is illusory, however, since the preponderant majority of human beings have categorically no choice whatever as to their work, either nowadays or in any previous day in history; where, as in America, the idea is entertained that there is such choice for some, the fact remains that choice in work is conditioned decisively by birth, heredity, privilege, environment or happenstance. The notion that some men enjoy actual freedom of choice in work (despite the persistent popularization of this view in the American sects and denominations) directly contradicts both common experience and the biblical insight that it is the *whole* of creation which is fallen and subjected to the power of death: not merely selected men, not nearly every man, but all of mankind; not just part of creation, not only most of it, but the whole of creation.

The concomitant idea that a man must assume the burden of work in order to be occasionally or eventually emancipated from it in leisure or retirement or enrichment is, of course, but a slightly modified version of the same illusion associated with the issue of choice in work in which it appears that there are persons or times or regions somehow exempted from the Fall. That there are no such people or occasions or places is the significance of the emphasis here upon the various forms of non-work as work.

There is no way in which the broken relationship which work represents can be transcended so as to avoid or mitigate or obviate the burden of that brokenness. It must be acknowledged, confronted, suffered and survived on its own terms, as it were, as the very aggression of death against life. What must be faced and felt, in the uttermost of a man's being, is that assault of the power of death feigning to be sovereign over life—over the particular life of a particular person and over all of existence throughout all of history.

It is, so to speak, only then and there—where there is no equivocation or escape possible from the fullness of death's vigor and brutality, when a man is exposed in absolute vulnerability—that life can be beheld and welcomed as the gift which life is. In *that* singular affection for life, death is transcended in a way in which dominion is restored to a man in his own life and in his relationships with the rest of creation.

Despite the profanity of what passes instead of worship in so many churchly sanctuaries, it is the restored dominion of men in creation which constitutes the genius of worship. And it is worship with such integrity in everyday life which supersedes the brokenness of work for a

mature human being (which is the only vocation to which a Christian is called). I had known
that before the illness and the pain. When I
could no longer distinguish work from non-
work, it had been because these had become, in
reality, worship, and their character as work or
non-work, with their implicit threats of death,
had been transcended. Now, in this disease, I
understood that the pain had become my work
and that the pain represented a familiar crisis
to be transcended by a grace also familiar.

After that, though the pain did not relent, I
was free of anxiety about my survival.

II SUCCOR

Lord, thou knowest all my desire; and
my groaning is not hid from thee.

My heart panteth, my strength hath failed me,
and the light of mine eyes is gone from me.

My lovers and my neighbors did stand looking
upon my trouble, and my kinsmen stood afar off.

Psalm 38:9–11

The therapy had failed during the summer of 1968 and the pain had taken its possession of me, and, by the breach of autumn, the issue had become not whether I would live or die, but when death would succeed. The diagnosis—that I suffered a pancreatic difficulty impairing the capability of utilizing food—had, by now, been repeatedly verified. The medical treatment had been conscientious. I had been a dutiful patient. Yet my condition consistently deteriorated: so steadily so that it became a necessary inference that there was some secret complication, some additional ailment undetected in hospital or laboratory.

Dr. Abramson, Block Island's general practitioner, was the first to mention to me the possibility of such an illusive danger. His bedside manner is blunt. He had had a regular surveillance of me during the months since I had been at the Roosevelt Hospital and had seen the gradual, relentless aggravation of my situation. "There must be something *else* wrong," he told me one afternoon when I had reported to him that the pain was deepening and that the remedies against the pain seemed to me virtually superfluous. He considered that my distress was distinguished from what would be expected from the disease which had been identified. "Maybe you have a cyst," he said, "that would account for this much pain." He paused a minute. "Of course, if you have one of them, it'll probably be fatal. The only way to find out is surgery, but it would probably be fatal anyway. They're usually fatal." His tone was so matter-of-fact that what he said did not scare me. And it certainly did not surprise me—I was dying and I knew it; my body had, so to speak, known that for a long time and, as that summer ended, my mind had lately confessed the same knowledge.

the somber options

There had been explored, somewhat earlier, the possibility of surgery; now that the therapy had failed and that suspicion of some complicating ailment had arisen, the question of an operation was reappraised. An eminent surgeon who was consulted concluded the risk so large that he would not undertake any procedure. Other professional counsel was divided, as were the views of those few friends in whom I entrusted the news of my ambiguous circumstances.

Ambiguity indeed! The alternatives confronting me were only unambiguous in that each appeared equally disagreeable. Surgery—provided a surgeon could be located who was both competent and audacious—posed the odds of whatever hidden ailment my body might conceal. Yet not to risk surgery courted a sudden calamity—should that secret illness mature—from which no doctor or medicine could retrieve life. Or, with scrutinous medical management, and

73

Job's own patience on my part, I could linger among the living for some indeterminate period —some months, most likely; perchance some years.

Theoretically there was another option: default. I could demur or I could deliberately refuse to decide. But these remained only theoretical possibilities for me because I knew that any form of default is a decision in itself: stupid or lazy or foolish or ignorant or cowardly, as the case may be, but nonetheless a decision bearing all the consequences and responsibility which accrue in premeditation. That default is effectually a decision, theologically speaking, simply means that default as much as calculation is subjected to God's judgment, which is the reason, I suppose, why in the confessionals in the Book of Common Prayer as much stress is placed upon the sin of men's omissions as upon that of commission. Default *is* decision—how often has that been dramatized in the agony of mankind? Within my own lifetime, the default typical of professed Christians in Nazi Germany had been culpable, along with other factors, for the incineration of the Jews. Even now, my own race and class in my own country—the white Anglo-Saxon Protestant Americans—have been so profoundly corrupted by their defaults, accumulated through generations, on the racial scene, that genocidal policies can actually be pursued by the State without either protest or compassion being roused among the white

majority, as has been seen in the massacres of
civilian children and women in Vietnam as well
as in the systematic police aggression against
the Black Panthers in a score of cities.

If default is efficacious for nations and races,
it is so also for persons, I knew, as could be seen
from the ignominious disposition of the disciples toward Christ, near the end. Default was
the stance toward Christ of the disciples at
Gethsemane. The people of the churches dwell
much upon Judas' betrayal and Peter's denial,
but the other disciples, when the crucial time
came, simply copped out.

Default feigns non-involvement in life as a
human being. Not every abstention is a default.
One can imagine or observe circumstances in
which someone's particular abstention is an intentional form of involvement. A rather cogent
argument could be maintained, for example,
that abstention from suffrage was a responsible
involvement for black citizens in the 1968 presidential election, given the alternatives embodied in the three candidates—Wallace's militant
hostility or Nixon's cynical commitments to
white racists or Humphrey's inept paternalism.
Such would be no default.

Default is no problem for wicked men: malice
precludes default. Default is a truly fatal temptation for men who otherwise may be regarded
as good, as the disciples exemplified. Default is
a temptation because it plagues men exactly at
the point of their anxiety for their moral inno-

75

cence. They suppose they will be morally harmed if they become involved and so they conjure up the illusion that they are not involved. Or else they rely upon their own ignorance or preoccupation as if it assured them unaccountability. Such temptation is fatal, manifestly, because to succumb to it is an abdication of humanness, a renunciation of life.

The ugly irony is that default is certain to be morally damaging to the one who defaults, whatever the moral risks of intentional involvement may be assessed to be. A corollary of that is that the empirical risks of involvement are almost always exaggerated. I recall visiting Columbia, South Carolina, some years ago, for instance, just after the disturbances attending the token integration of the University of Mississippi by James Meredith. Some of the clergy there had induced the Law School of the University of South Carolina to invite me to deliver a lecture on civil disobedience. As astonished as gratified to have access to such a forum in such a place, I went to Columbia, gave a lecture, which was substantially the same as one I had previously made at the Cornell Law School, and spent three days on the campus there. At that time it was known that an attempt would be made to tokenly integrate the University of South Carolina during the ensuing year. Those who opposed this were, at the time of my visit, energetically preparing for the violent obstruction of the attempt. It was reported to me by some fraternity men that guns and other weapons were being stashed away in the frats. There was some evidence that the local White Citizens Councils had financed the placement of some boys as students in the university for the purpose of rioting or other disruption when the time for integration came. Another Mississippi situation—or worse—was in the making. And the only folk who appeared to be active and involved were the aggressive racists or their mercenaries.

My lecture at the law school, which was the same in South Carolina as it had been in the North, had sought to distinguish civil disobedience by passive resistance or other non-violent tactics, which uphold the rule of law while opposing particular laws, then exemplified by Martin Luther King or Medgar Evers, from more radical forms of civil disobedience that subvert the rule of law as such—specifically, the terrorism, typified at that time by the activities of the White Citizens Councils, or the abuse of process by law-enforcement authorities, or the evasion or manipulation of the law by racial or class factions, both of the latter were and remain commonplace in South and North alike. In the days which followed my address, I found myself being sought out privately and individually by various faculty, students and administrators. Each, as it turned out, bore the same message. Each had heard my remarks and wanted to indicate that each had found them agreeable, but each complained that he was the only person in Columbia so persuaded. Enough came to see me—about forty different persons—so that the protest of each—that he was a lonely and hence necessarily silent dissenter in such a place—was exposed as absurd. The people of these sentiments may not have constituted a majority on that campus, but there were obviously a significant number and some of them were persons of influential stature in the university, and clearly there was no basis in fact for their individual feelings of isolation and no reason for them to be silent for fear of being the only voice. I was able to cause some of them to appreciate this and, from their discovery of one another and their concerted witness, along with other factors, South Carolina was spared the trauma Ole Miss had suffered when token integration happened, while my Columbia friends were saved from an especially ignominious default.

an adolescent decision

The issue of default is not the only aspect of decision-making which has intrigued me; from adolescence I had been at once fascinated and bothered by the means through which a man decides. While in my early teens I rejected, albeit with very great effort and with a certain passion which has never departed from me, the simplistic notion of decisions being mere choices between self-evident good and evil. That conception of both personal and social decisions had very great prominence in the white Anglo-Saxon Protestant America of my upbringing. It was part of the indoctrination of schoolchildren. It was the cornerstone (instead of the Bible) in the instruction of the young in church. It was part of the prevalent family ethic among whites, although, mercifully, within my own family it had been challenged by the Depression experience and my own parents had a better sense of the moral ambiguity of human circumstances than did many others.

My own realization of ambiguity and my emphatic repudiation of moral simplistics came, as might have been anticipated, in the making of an actual decision: I decided, at fourteen, not to become a priest.

The parish church had been a more than routine part of my childhood; it was at least as central as school in terms of its claims upon time, interest and loyalty. There were not only the conventional programs of the parish in which to participate—the services, church school, a young people's fellowship, the acolyte's guild—but the parish premises and the rectory were places where I spent other hours —playing, doing errands and odd jobs, loitering, watching. I was religiously precocious, read much about religion, and pursued long and sometimes esoteric religious discussions with the clergy. This religiosity, as I now see it, became focused and personified in my relationship with one of the priests of the parish and, after a time, I found myself being much urged by him to decide upon the priesthood as a vocation. I do not know—and, fortunately, I am not the judge in the matter—how that minister reguarded our relationship. I do not know his motives, and I no longer care what they may have been, whatever they may have been. I do not think he had a serious appreciation of what was happening to me in my side of our encounter. What was happening was a gradual intensification of pressures upon me to decide to be a priest and to thereby emulate him. Some-how, from him, the impression came to me that it was only by being ordained that it would be vouchsafed that I was a Christian, indeed, only in that way that it was sure that any man was a Christian.

I was, for a long time, assailed by the multiple ambiguities attending this decision. I had an al-most overwhelming sense of being possessed and, thus, coerced, and I harbored the premoni-tion that to choose to be a priest, or even to undertake the steps in collegiate and seminary education which would make me a postulant under coercion of any sort would be intolerable. Another pressure was economic; my family, never well-to-do, had been impoverished in the Depression years, during which I had been born, and, like other working-class families, had little economic security much less resources for my education beyond secondary school. I un-derstood that if I made a commitment to the priesthood, the financial barriers to college and graduate study could be overcome without bur-den to my parents. Religion beguiled me, but I was also beginning to comprehend that the Gospel was, somehow, not about religion, but reached beyond religion. That caused a strong resistance intellectually and emotionally within me to this idea that this influential priest had managed, whether inadvertently or by design, to communicate to me—that to be a priest was the seal of the Christian life and that the priest-

81

hood embodied a higher or better or more conscientious or more certain disposition of one's life as a Christian.

That a priest was in any sense more exalted than any other person, in the life of the Gospel in the world, could not be true. And if a priest were that in the life of the Church, then it could only betray something profoundly false in the Church. That was my decision. It was made fiercely—more than likely because I was only in my early teens at the time. *I would be damned if I would be a priest.* That was what I decided. I would not be a priest and, moreover, I would spend my life refuting any who suppose that to be serious about the Christian faith required ordination. I would be a Christian in spite of the priesthood, in spite of all the priests, in spite of this priest who had, as I saw it at the time, importuned me.

Spite is the right word; it was a good many years before my hostility toward the priesthood as an institution and an occupation and my sensitivity against the particular priest I have mentioned abated. They were years in which I excelled in the politics of the churches and of their youth and student movements. Within one of those years, at the height of my career as a student Christian, I presided at the first national ecumenical student conference, was prominent in the United Christian Youth Movement, served as vice-chairman of the National Student YMCA, headed the New England Student

Christian Movement, was chairman of the National Student Christian Federation, represented Episcopalian youth at the World Conference of Christian Youth, and American students at the World's Student Christian Federation. I was proving, I suppose, that one could be recognized as a Christian without being a priest or a candidate for the priesthood. I was becoming a professional Christian without the conventional and supposedly necessary credential of professional Christians—ordination. I was becoming a pharisee. That my situation was pathetic and incongruous, in the context of the Gospel, had not yet dawned on me. That, in truth, I was no Christian as such at the time, or that I can only be said to have become a Christian later in my life, in radically different circumstances, and yet was known as a super-Christian is evidence of the ferocity of my adolescent decision. That was as well a measure of the ambiguity of the whole of the event of the decision not to be a priest.

decision and judgment

As decisions are evaluated conventionally, this early and negative one seemed, when it was made and subsequently, to be a large decision, one with consequences both privately significant and remarkably far reaching, and a milestone morally in my life. At the least, many things which later happened to me were portended, if not anticipated, by it, and it would be simple for me to attribute a momentous status autobiographically to this young decision. In my most lucid moments, however, I know that this is a romantic and misleading comprehension of the particular decision as well as a confused and false conception of the reality of decision-making. The truth is that decisions do not vary either quantitatively or qualitatively. It may seem to a person, as it may to observers, that certain decisions are great, and the remainder of them trivial, but actually every decision is of equal import and potential. Similarly, there are not some decisions which are morally significant, while the rest are morally innocuous, but all decisions are moral decisions. Charles Williams somewhere makes the same point when he writes of the mere lighting of a cigarette being a cosmic event, one in which the essential issue of existence itself is symbolized even though the act appears casual and inconsequential. Contemporary medical information about so small and vulgar a decision as having a cigarette gives Williams' illustration of the cosmic incarnate in the apparently commonplace frightening veracity.

People—myself included—are adept at misconstruing the size and moral scope of their own decisions because the event of decision poses the issue of judgment—concretely, the judgment of God. Apprehensive about that mystery, human beings are anxious to circumscribe the realm of God's judgment as much as possible where, indeed, they cannot feign to circumvent God's judgment altogether. By imagining that only select decisions risk judgment, men delude themselves about their own moral standing, which is to say, about their humanity. The person who thinks that only some decisions are moral decisions or that there be occasional great decisions amongst many trivial decisions is engaged in trying to confine God's judgment in history to those matters about which he is morally self-confident. Reference to God at all, on this scene, becomes silly: if God's judgment is operative according to the way in which men discriminate as to their decisions, then God is generically irrelevant, immobilized as any influence in human affairs, a pawn of men's guile, or just an august name for rationalization or self-deception.

That God's name is subjected to such abuse does not bother me (Why should it? In the biblical witness, it does not bother God.) except where it has become a principle of religion among professed believers, as it has, to a great extent, in Protestant denominationalism and in precouncilor American Catholicism. In these contexts it represents a radical apostasy denying the consistency of God's vocation as judge in our day as much as in the biblical saga, and reducing God from sovereign of creation to some absurd creature, bereft of either independence or freedom, a servant of human vanity and convenience.

I speak here of God's judgment in relation to decisions of persons, but I affirm much the same with regard to decisions of institutions, especially those of nations. That is familiarly documented in war, where each side finds its cause to be the will of God. It is, for Americans, gruesomely dramatized in Vietnam, where the initial involvement and the subsequent escalations were so vainglorious, so certain of the commendation of God's judgment upon the nation, so assertedly righteous that, now, to extricate the country's troops and wealth from the misadventure not only taxes the credibility of the nation but also ridicules the probity of God.

87

So conceived, of course, God is not God at all, but an idol—a figment of human imagination or delusion or a handy synonym for human rationalization or, where principalities are concerned, a product of tradition or folkway or a convenient symbol for elemental self-interest.

In biblical perspective, God as judge is more fearsome, more holy, and more credible. Biblically, God alone is judge, solitary and exclusive in His prerogative, beyond appeasement by any man or any nation. To His judgment, there are no qualifications or exemptions: He judges all men and all things, every decision, every action, every thought, every omission; neither sparrows nor a hair on the head are neglected in judgment. God's judgment is *His* knowledge, not to be apprehended or imitated by men or by institutions. His judgment is His secret. No man, no nation, no creature whatever has even a clue as to how he or it is judged in any matter: God's judgment is utterly secret. His judgment is in time and yet in the consummation of time; His judgment is contemporary but also transcendent; His judgment encompasses all that was, all that is, all that is to be, as if it all were a single event which, in the end, it is.

Still, though none know anything of God's judgment of particular deeds or decisions, much has been made known in the world of the *character* of God's judgment, and that notably, if not exclusively, in the history of Israel, which, in this reference, includes the ministry of Jesus as

the climactic happening in Israel's sojourn.
Thus we behold a coincidence of mercy in
God's judgment. Forgiveness displaces and
abolishes punishment in God's judgment. Repentance thereby counts as righteousness in
God's judgment. All of this is familiar enough
biblically, and it is also discernible in common
life. It can be seen, analogically, for instance, in
the American racial crisis as the attitudes and
positions of white vs. black have altered with
the changes of personality and strategy that
have occurred in the last decade. The whites,
at the time—that some have belatedly come to a
better mind does not eradicate the earlier fact
—of Martin Luther King's dominance in the
black revolt, consistently responded to King's
non-violent tactics with grave hostility and,
much more often than not, violence cloaked in
legality. That white hostility sanctioned the assassination of Dr. King and condones the abuse
of the law by which the truth of the murder is
suppressed. Today, to the white mentality, the
black revolt means the Black Panthers, whom
the whites have been told by the public authorities threaten revolutionary upheaval, and
whose rhetoric is unabashedly provocative to
white ears. The response to the Panthers is a
white hostility authorizing systematic, official
repression culminating in genocide. I suggest
that the white hostility to Dr. King and the
white hostility to the Black Panthers are morally
distinguishable, and, indeed, despite all the superficial similarities, radically different. The

white rejection of Dr. King was a guilt-ridden hostility; Dr. King persisted in threatening to forgive American whites, which meant that when he confronted them, they gazed upon their corporate guilt as a people. In the face of that, whites had either to truly repent or to destroy, somehow, this man whose very existence certified the guilt. By contrast, in addition to the official slander circulated among whites about them, the Black Panthers do address whites as "mother fuckers" (which I regard less as a profanity than as a name with decadent connotations befitting the pathology of the white majority) and do speak, at times, of retribution. So, as they see it, insulted and endangered by the Panthers, whites feel fully justified in their hostility and the aggression which it condones against the Panthers. The Panthers do not promise to forgive whites, they offer enmity and strife for persecution and oppression, they tender tit for tat, and thereby they allow whites to evade their inherited guilt and to suppose that whites harbor only a righteous anger toward blacks. In the latter is the only kind of judgment within the capabilities of human beings or races or nations—it is a perverse, self-serving, fallen "judgment" no matter how much it is embellished with the name of God. But in the dialectic of white violence and Dr. King's radical prescience—his commitment to forgiveness—is a glimpse of the very grace characteristic of God's own judgment of the world.

decision as vocational event

It is the ubiquity of God's judgment—extending to every time and place—and the universality of God's judgment—reaching every man and every principality or power—and the secrecy of God's judgment—which embraces all creation—taken together with such knowledge as there is of the character of God's judgment—namely that His judgment is a facet of His grace—that authorizes the emphasis of Saint Paul on the extraordinary freedom of the Christian, in making decisions, from anxiety about how those decisions are judged by God. Paul redundantly boasts that men are not the judges of one another, that the State is not the judge, that the company of the Church is not the judge, that he as an Apostle is not the judge, that a man is, least of all, his own judge. And Paul considers the presumption to judge, on the part of institutions or men, a moral dissipation. Genesis, incidentally, affirms the same truth. A nation that usurps God's office as judge vitiates its own authority as a nation. A man cannot play judge,

91

even of himself, without suffering profound corruption in his identity as a human being.

Not to be judge and not to judge, and not to be subjected to judgment by other men, or principalities, describes, as Paul well knew, the freedom to decide this or that in grace—in fear and trembling—in the audacity which takes the place of anxiety over one's moral justification. It is the maximal freedom that a human being can experience. It is, for human beings, the definitive freedom, showing both the most mature humanity and the proper limits of the institutional powers. And if there be complaint that such a remarkable freedom, when practiced, causes perpetual revolution in all things, then let the complaint stand as a fair designation of how the Gospel sets forth the vocation to be human.

That is, of course, what is really at the heart of decision. Decision is a vocational event.

The maturing of the ecumenical movement has been associated in the past decade, in most of the churches in this country, with a widespread and lively discussion of vocation as an issue for the laity, while, during the same time, the religious orders and the clergy have suffered a reappraisal of the meaning of vocation, which has been agonizingly dramatized in the decline of seminary enrollment, the decrease in admissions to orders and in candidacies for ordination, the proliferation of so-called experimental non-parochial ministries—both with and without ec-

clesiastical sanction, the vigorous challenge to
celibacy as a prerequisite in the Roman priesthood, along with innumerable drop-outs and
other departures. Happily, to me, as I recollect
my young decision against ordination and the
circumstances surrounding it, these recent de-
velopments represent a radical and wholesome
departure from the inherited stereotype of the
ordained ministry, or the religious orders, as the
only options for "full-time" vocation. Still, for
all the attention there has been to the wider
scope of Christian vocation, the idea of vocation
remains too much and too often wedded to the
choice of occupation or profession. The work
a person does—and the choice of his work, insofar as it may be ever said that a choice exists—
is, manifestly, vocationally significant, but work
is never to be equated with vocation. Moreover, as has been previously mentioned, the relationships pertinent in the various forms of non-
work, in this society, theologically have the
meaning of work and morally are the equivalent
of work. To consider vocation only in its relevance to a job, in an era in which mandatory
and progressively younger retirement—compul-
sory or practically necessary—and increasingly
longer education, and unresolved problems of
technological unemployment and sociological
unemployability are among the conditions which
fill most of a person's lifetime, issues in an extremely truncated, and necessarily distorted
comprehension of vocation. The temptation,

now, is not that vocation will become falsely restricted to specified occupations, as had been the case in earlier days, but that vocation will be identified only with work in a narrow sense of employment and the like, and that the much longer years of childhood and school or of retirement and leisure or, for the poor, of joblessness and welfare dependency will be regarded as vocational vacuums.

Biblically, vocation does not have any connotation limited to work. Vocation pertains to the whole of life, including work, of course, if and when there is work, but embracing every other use of time, every other engagement of body or mind, every other circumstance in life. In the Gospel, vocation does not mean being professionally religious, it has no special reference to the ecclesiastical occupations, it does not imply "full-time Christian service" (as some preachers still put it), it does not require extemporizing prayer into business and political situations—especially at breakfast time—it has nothing to do as such with philanthropy—tax deductible or otherwise; it is not about honesty, sobriety, thrift, loyalty or similar homely virtues on the job, it does not concern positive attitudes and is alien to the success ethic. Moreover, in the Gospel, vocation always bears an implication of immediacy—there is really no such thing as preparing to undertake one's vocation when one grows up or when one graduates or when one obtains a certain position or when one gets

94

to a certain place. Vocation is always here and now, without anxiety where one might be tomorrow, what regard there is for tomorrow and tomorrow's issues are sufficiently anticipated, so far as vocation is concerned, in today's unconditional involvement in life as it is. Vocation has to do with recognizing life as a gift and honoring the gift in living. To that, the question of whether another day will be added to one's life, and, if that comes to pass, how the gift will be spent on the morrow, is a distraction or diversion from living of the gift today. Carried, as the *Letter of James* cautions, too far, a concern about how to live faithfully tomorrow causes infidelity in living today. Carried to its ultimate absurdity, the anxiety for tomorrow becomes a preoccupation with a fantasy afterlife, a notion without biblical support, albeit popularized in churches, at the cost of squandering or repudiating the immediate gift of life.

In the Gospel, vocation means being a human being, now, and being neither more, nor less than a human being, now. And, thus, is the vocation of other men illuminated and affirmed, and so also is the vocation of the institutional powers and the principalities of this world exposed and upheld. And, thus, each and every decision, whether it seems great or small, whether obviously or subtly a moral problem, becomes and is a vocational event, secreting, as it were, the very issue of existence.

an ordinary and common experience

My state of mind, when it became apparent
that the therapy had failed and that the practical options open to me were limited and, in each
case, both disagreeable and dangerous, was informed privately chiefly by the terms with which
I had come to deal with the pain—that pain is not
something extraordinary or abnormal but the
same reality as work, the concrete experience of
fallenness—and by my understanding of the vocational character of decision. It was a state of
mind freed, in this way, from potential hang-ups
of all sorts. That is to say, I knew that there
was nothing traumatic, nothing heroic, nothing
tragic, nothing stoic, nothing dramatic in my
situation. In truth, mine was a commonplace
experience, not only in relation to the circumstances of other human beings, but also in relation to my own history. I realized I had to make
some decision, but it was as if I had already
rehearsed that decision one million times whenever I had theretofore made any decision about
anything. Moreover, I knew that it did not mat-

ter what my decision would be vocationally. The decision might well affect how long I survived, it certainly would affect the physiology of my survival, but neither of these matters altered the vocational issue, which is to live as a human being while one lives. Nor did survival, for whatever time and in whatever health, change the moral significance of my decision, since that pertains to God's own judgment, about which I could only confess ignorance, together with a confidence in His mercy.

With this outlook, the decision was made, and quite matter-of-factly, without excitement, lucidly, unanxious about any future, almost casually. I would have surgery.

I felt like a human being. I felt free.

the reality of prayer

In the midst of death, I felt free, with a surety and composure which, while not wholly novel to my experience, was more thorough and sustained than I had previously enjoyed.

Encircled by the manifoldness of death—the death so impatiently at work in my own body; the death so militant in my own country; the death so idolized by my own race; the death which seems to be the moral sovereign in the world; the death incarnate in all existence everywhere (which the Old Testament calls the Fall) —I felt alive: very much alive: never more alive.

This whole experience throughout the months of distress, progressive disease, failing therapy, excruciation, and, at last, decision, could be described as prayer. I am hesitant to do so, though I clearly believe that is the accurate description, because the event of prayer, certain acts called prayer, the very word "prayer" have gathered such ridiculous associations. That is not only the case with the obscene performances, which pass as public prayer, at inaugurations, in

99

locker rooms, before Rotary luncheons, and in many churchly sanctuaries, but also the practice of private prayer is attended by gross profanity, the most primitive superstitions, and sentimentality which is truly asinine.

I would hope, here, in designating this experience of mine as prayer that the reader would greet the term disabused of any such spooky or sickly preconceptions about the reality of prayer; I would wish the reader to follow these remarks about prayer as if he had never before heard of the subject.

Part of the prevalent misunderstanding of prayer, and a crucial reason for the widespread corruption of prayer in practice, is a startling confusion, originating in American Protestantism, but infecting Catholicism and Judaism in America to an appreciable extent, as to the distinction between prayer and worship. The familiar notion virtually equates the two. I observe that most Protestants—specifically, most white Protestants of the denominations and sects with an American genesis (the issue is far less aggravated in the liturgical traditions of European origins that have been transplanted in the United States or in black Christendom in America)—conceive of worship, at most, as a combination of prayer plus preaching, organized, more often than not, as interludes in a choir's performance. Music—including the music of choirs—along with preaching—*if* it is an exposition of the biblical Word in the contemporary scene and

idiom—along with prayer—*if* what be practiced
be prayer—all have an appropriate presence in
worship, but the mere conjunction of the three,
or any possible combinations thereof, does not
constitute worship.

Worship is the celebration of life in its
totality. Worship is the sacramental appropria-
tion of all of life in celebration. Worship is the
festival of creation. Organized public corporate
worship is a theatrical restoration of creation in
which each and all of the participants symbolically and ritually enjoy their own selves and one
another and all things. Liturgical worship, which
is inherently a communal event, whether formal
or spontaneous, whether traditional or extemporaneous, is an esoteric portrayal of the reconciliation of the whole world. Worship is the
celebration of life in its ultimate expectancy.
Sacramental worship is always, hence, profoundly ethical and specifically and self-
consciously eschatological in its ethics, exposing
contemporary society—whatever its current es-
tate, whenever it is, wherever it happens to be—
to the Gospel's eagerness for the end and
fulfillment of history in God. In turn, that
means that worship is explicitly a political and
social happening of the most radical dimensions, illuminating every flaw and injustice,
every falsity and offense, every vanity and need
of the prevailing social order while notoriously,
passionately, incessantly calling for the over-

turning—or, more literally, the transfiguring—of the incumbent order in society.

Much more may be affirmed of worship, but suffice to say, in order to distinguish prayer from worship, that worship has its most telling analogues in common life in revolution, on the one hand, and in play, on the other.

And though, here, the focus is upon corporate public worship, parallel affirmations are in order as to the worship of men dispersed in the world, of the worship which prefigures vocation, of the worship which symbolizes restored dominion for men in creation, as has been elsewhere discussed.

Prayer is not inappropriate in worship, so understood and so performed, of course, but the two should not be identified, oversimply, as the same thing. Where prayer and worship are heedlessly equated, the integrity of each is impaired, and the enhancement that each can bring to human life is diluted.

Let it be clear, parenthetically, that no challenge is brought here to the sincerity with which men, in various fashions, suppose they pray. That is wholly irrelevant to whether or not supposed prayer is prayer within the purview of the Gospel.

Any number of different exercises are deemed to be prayer which do not possess the dignity of prayer and, in certain instances, actually contradict the reality of prayer. The confusion and, as the case may be, the corruption centers upon the alleged interest of God in prayer and, indeed, upon the matter of whether, in some machinations men call prayer, God could possibly be privy to the activity at all.

An illusion, at least, of reciprocity between men and God is maintained where prayer is construed as a way in which men "talk with God," or, otherwise, literally communicate with Him, and where the presumption is that God is, somewhere, passively implicated—listening to this talk. Often, with the same general conception of prayer, God's attributed role is enlarged: He is said not only to listen but also to answer in some manner. Some people boast that God speaks to them as if they really mean that they hear God verbalizing in direct address to themselves; others are content to assign to selected events subsequent to prayer answers besought of God; still others find prayer to be an effort to persuade God to permit what they desire, and the attainment of the goal or gain desired becomes God's answer, while a failure in such attainment can either be blamed on a deficient zeal in the arts of persuasion or upon God's well-known inscrutability.

What is suspect in each of the foregoing styles of prayer, what they share in common, is the definitive emphasis upon human initiative in prayer. In each of them, prayer is a primary act of men, as to which either God is a passive object or, one might say, a victim, or else God is a mere respondent of some sort. Whatever the case, the initiative—that which constitutes and characterizes and consummates the happening— is never with God, but always with men. That makes God, in prayer, of all things, a dependent upon human attentions and overtures. And that makes a mockery of God as He is biblically known—as God is beheld and esteemed, for one notable example, when Jesus utters the Lord's Prayer.

What is offensive in each of these arts which usurp prayer to biblical experience— remembering that the biblical experience embraces both the saga of the people of God in the biblical times and the sojourn of biblical men in the present day—is their debasement of God. "Prayer" which relegates God to passivism or to mechanical or magical responses to human maneuvering and manipulating issues in a denial of God's godliness—of God's otherness, as Karl Barth put it—of God's freedom as God. Such a humiliation of God, even though it is not accomplished by men self-consciously, points to a real profanity rampant in this land, especially in churches, and also in the precincts of what some have called America's civic religion, where, quite literally, God's name is taken in vain.

What is further suspect about practices called prayer such as these is that God, in any meaningful sense in which the name of God may be used, is not an essential party to what transpires at all, but that the invocation of God's name provides a suitably vague and aptly euphoric concealment of some other transaction, which may range from autosuggestion to motivational manipulation to hallucination to astrological calculation to voodoo incantation to sorcery, which bears a general characteristic as an act of self-generation.

Notice that I do not deny that any of these indulgences—they were so condemned by Saint Paul in Galatians—may yield the results sought, or be somehow efficacious so far as the practitioner is concerned, and I repeat that I do not raise now, at all, any doubt about the sincerity of anyone. The query I have concerns whether what is involved is prayer as prayer has meaning in the Gospel of Jesus Christ. At the heart of *that* issue is the fact that in these varieties of alleged prayer, God turns out to be a projection of the will or whim (or lust or delusion) of the one who "prays."

Yet if what has been performed in white Protestantism, and to some extent elsewhere, as prayer is not prayer, in a sense which is conscientious about the Gospel, but instead witchcraft or hypnosis or positive thinking or some similar hocus-pocus, then, what is prayer?

Prayer is a relationship which God initiates and constitutes between Himself and men. It is God's action in prayer which is definitive: God enables men to pray. Prayer is not something which, so to speak, begins with men and ends with God, but throughout prayer, men are respondents and, more than that, the possibility of

the human response to God called prayer is bestowed by God's initiative.

The substance of that initiative is God's incessant, patient, and ubiquitous affirmation of His
own creation, including, concretely, human beings in relation to the rest of creation and,
now, the particular person—who prays—in this
relation to creation. The latter should be em-
phasized: there is an integrity in God's affirmation of His own creation, which requires that the
affirmance of a specific man always places that
man at the interstices of the whole of creation.
There is no way in which a specific person can
suffer the affirmation of his own life by God in a
void, without connection to all other men and
all other things and, indeed, all of time, which
is why incidentally, the Book of Common
Prayer makes reference to praying in the company of the Communion of Saints. It is also why
a radically individualistic conception of prayer
—such as Norman Vincent Peale merchandises
—oriented toward personal success (an occurrence which can *never* happen except at the
expense of other human beings) is not prayer
in accordance with biblical experience and is
accurately classified as sorcery.

The essential response of men in prayer is
always the same, regardless of how, in an instance, it may be symbolized verbally or ac-
tively; the response is always a confession of
human creatureliness. Prayer originates in God's
affirmation of life for the one who prays in the

context of the totality of existence, and prayer is consummated in participation of the one who prays in that very same affirmation. Because prayer has such dimensions as these, it is not superstitious or otherwise nonsensical to speak of God already knowing all our needs and desires before we ask, or of prayer being answered even before a prayer is uttered. Because prayer has its consistent focus, for both God and men, in God's affirmation of particular life, and of all of life, prayer (rather than being a technique for bolstering willpower, generating willfulness or aggrandizing ambition—as Dr. Peale advertises) always entreats the perfection of God's will by the fulfillment of your will or my will in the acceptance of our humanity as such. Thus the biblical archetype of prayer sums up all that transpires in such a phrase as "nevertheless, thy will be done, O Lord," and these words are then not some way of tricking ourselves or trying to con God.

One of the implications of prayer construed as human participation in God's affirmation of life is that prayer is not inherently verbal. In a culture which is verbally adept, not to mention one which is verbose, like America, it is to be expected that the verbalization of prayer would be common and customary. I do not doubt that putting prayer into words can be edifying. I also believe that the redundant use of verbal formularies in prayer can help maintain a sense of continuity in what I have here named the biblical experience of prayer. Besides, contemporary Christians ought to feel at home amidst the Communion of Saints and, where the ritual verbalization of prayer assists that, I am glad. A problem arises, however, where words are taken as so specialized and important in themselves that their mere use is equated with prayer or where the words are supposed to be intrinsically efficacious. That is one of the points at which the line is traversed between prayer and the practice of sorcery.

Without discounting a legitimate verbal usage in prayer, but remembering that words are perhaps the most elementary symbols which can be appropriated in prayer, it remains basic that prayer designates a state of being of the one who prays or of the company which prays that, in given circumstances, may or may just as well not be verbalized. That prayer is not inherently verbal is disclosed more fully where such a state of being becomes and is, with more or less intensity from day to day, the continuing disposition of a person. Then, of course, where there *is* verbalization, the vocabulary of prayer becomes marvelously versatile and literally any words may be appropriate: familiar or novel, traditional or spontaneous, solemn or silly. Indeed, ecstatic speech, speaking in tongues, incomprehensible to either speaker or hearer, can then be a means of prayer.

When I write that my own situation in those months of pain and decision can be described as prayer, I do not only recall that during that time I sometimes read the Psalms and they became *my* psalms, or that, as I have also mentioned, I occasionally cried "Jesus" and that name was my prayer, but I mean that I also at times would shout "Fuck!" and that was no obscenity, but a most earnest prayerful utterance.

In the final analysis, no matter what the vocabulary of prayer, or where muteness displaces words in prayer, the content—what is communicated by a man in the world before God—in prayer is in each and every circumstance the same and it can be put plainly in one word: *Help!* That is the word of Gethsemane's prayer; that is the word of the Lord's Prayer; that is the prayer when Christ repeats the Twenty-second Psalm from the cross.

It is the prayer of Christ interceding for all men, and it is the prayer of man as creature acknowledging God's vocation in affirming the life which He has called into being. It has been and is my prayer: it was, in the autumn of 1968, my prayer, that is to say, my condition, at once pathetic and glorious.

III   RECALL

When I am in heaviness, I will think upon God;
when my heart is vexed, I will complain.

Thou holdest mine eyes waking: I am so feeble
that I cannot speak.

I have considered the days of old, and the
years that are past.

I call to remembrance my song, and in the
night I commune with mine own heart, and search
out my spirit.

Psalm 77:3–6

My decision to risk surgery remained contingent upon locating a surgeon with the experience and skill requisite and, perhaps more crucial, with the courage to undertake an operation of greater than the usual uncertainties, the whole issue having been clouded, by now, by grave suspicions that, complicating the ailment detected and diagnosed at Roosevelt Hospital, there was some hidden trouble. I had talked with the Island physician about this, and I had consulted Dr. James Gabriel, in whose care I had been at Roosevelt and since. Some of my darker misgivings about the devotion of the American medical profession to an ethics of exploitation and greed, instead of an ethic of health and service, stemming, in part, from the episode with the dilettante doctor who had almost succeeded in invaliding me and who, in time, would almost certainly have achieved my death, had been tempered by my experience with Dr. Abramson on Block Island and Dr. Gabriel in New York City. I trusted Dr. Abramson and valued his bluntness; I had been much reassured by Dr. Gabriel's manifest medical competence and by his civility as a human being, as well.

I also besought the counsel of a friend, Dr. Robert Klopstock, himself a gifted chest surgeon, responsible for significant new procedures in that field, and a distinguished doctor. I had met and come to know Robert and his wife, Giselle, affectionately while the three of us were communicants in the same congregation in the city. The Klopstocks had come to this country in flight from the disaster which Nazism had wrought in their native Hungary. The inquiries of both Dr. Gabriel and Robert quite independently of each other—providentially, I suppose it might be said—yielded the same name: Dr. Milton Porter. Dr. Porter, who is chief of staff at Columbia-Presbyterian Medical Center in New York, had made a specialization in pancreatic disorders and qualified as one of perhaps three surgeons on the whole continent to whom my case could, with any degree of common sense, be entrusted. I saw Dr. Porter, and he saw me, and he would do it. He had lately been developing a new procedure, which theretofore had been performed nineteen times, with promising results. For me, the Porter procedure seemed to come as close as anything in sight to a possible remedy; in fact it appeared to be the only possible remedy, regardless of whatever booking odds might be computed on it. For Dr.

Porter, I gathered, dealing with my condition would furnish additional experience in this specific work he had begun and might provide some new knowledge. So my decision for surgery was ratified; a date—November 22—was set for the event.

a matter of providence?

If this commitment on Dr. Porter's part, as well as mine, accorded with common sense in the circumstances, there were nonetheless non-rational factors which influenced me, which I can recognize, though I do not admit to fully understanding them.

A patient's subjective attitude toward his doctor is, obviously, of immense significance in the whole story of illness, treatment and cure. Within my immediate experience—in this sickness—that subjectivity had become especially prominent, so much so that had I not been able to relate humanly, in an affirming way, with those who attended me as doctors, then their technical proficiency medically or surgically would have been, I think, neutralized. I found, in first meeting him, that I liked Dr. Porter as a person. Moreover, I soon learned enough about him to admire him. I discovered, for example, that with the establishment of medicare and medicaid, which commercial medicine had so vehemently opposed and which so very many entrepreneurs in the medical profession have sapped for profits, Dr. Porter caused a foundation to be established at Columbia-Presbyterian to which the hospital staff contributes medicare fees now received in cases where, prior to this, no fees at all were paid. The foundation's resources are expended in research and, thus, a double mileage is gained from the medicare funds. I call that admirable, particularly when contrasted with the phony charges and over-charges by which those in medicine as a business have sought to enrich themselves through medicare and medicaid, not to again mention the familiar, parallel scandals in private insurance schemes like Blue Cross and Blue Shield.

My early esteem for Dr. Porter—which has never been disappointed—was enhanced, in a peculiar way, by the fact that years before he and I had been contemporaries on the East Harlem scene, he working at Dr. Beatrice Berle's medical clinic, while I was living and practicing law on East One Hundredth Street. We had not become acquainted at the time, nothing having happened in the course of our respective involvements in the ghetto to bring us into contact. To meet now, as surgeon and patient, in somewhat desperate circumstances, after having been in such close proximity before, counted with me as more than an odd coincidence and, maybe, as no coincidence at all. It was, whatever else might be thought of

it, an edifying omen because it told me much
about Milton Porter as a man, as well as a doctor. Giselle Klopstock, who is a wise person
and who possesses intuitive faculties which are
remarkable, is the only one, prior to the operation, in whom I confided that I had some conviction, albeit illusive and undefined, about the
events which had culminated in my becoming
Dr. Porter's patient, especially about the East
Harlem background that we, unbeknownst, had
shared. Giselle declared it a matter of providence.

I did not quarrel with her conclusion when
we had that conversation, partly because
Giselle had spoken it with an authority for
which I have respect and in part because I had
no alternative suggestion that seemed appropriate. Providence is a strange conception. I have
some understanding, I think, of what is not
providence; I am not so sure I know what providence is. Often, it seems to me, it is one of
those terms used to cover what is inexplicable
even though no explanation can be maintained
about what it means—somewhat after the fash-
ion in which preachers invoke the name of the
Holy Spirit to fill voids in which they truth-
fully have nothing coherent to say. Anyway,
providence is different from coincidence,
though there are apparent similarities. I suppose that anything which can be said to be co-
incidental, can also be called providential, but
that does imply that the two are synonyms and

some happenings considered providential would not be sufficiently designated as mere coincidence. There is not, for one thing, the connotation of fortuity, of chance, of the erratic or of the casual in the idea of providence, and that, of course, has most force as a distinction between the two where a specific coincidence was such that it might readily also be referred to as luck.

Some of the notions, which are traditional, regrettably, within the American churches, conceive of the providential as the disclosure of that which God has foreordained. Such views presuppose that God has a "plan"—usually, elaborately detailed and highly personalized—which is "providentially" unfolded, but that makes God a kind of extraordinary bureaucrat and that robs men of the very freedom which is the distinctive humanizing characteristic. Regret enters that any convictions of the sort flourish in the churches because, with respect to both God and human beings, they corrupt biblical faith, making the relationship between God and men mechanical, manipulative and, incidentally, dull. Gone is the excitement of God's presence in human history; gone is the surprise of God's passion for common life; gone is the joy of worship which is spontaneous and voluntary; gone is love in men's response to God and to one another; gone, in a word, is that attribute of God and benefit for mankind about which the biblical witness is most insistent: grace.

Perhaps that is the clue to the biblical context of providence: grace. Perhaps we err or become confused about what providential means because we dwell upon only some particular event, an occasional occurrence that seems outstanding; we tend to think of the providential as rare and exceptional; we make selections, among all the things that happen to us, calling some matters of providence and treating the rest as having nothing to do with providence. Perhaps there just is no discrimination at all, in the concern of God for this life in this world, between one happening and another. *Perhaps everything is providential.*

If everything *is* providential, then providence means the constant and continual renewal of God's grace in all situations for every man throughout time. If everything is providential, then providence refers to God's capacity and His willingness to redeem all of life. It means that no circumstances ever arise which are beyond God's care or reach. It means that the power and reality of death at work concretely in the world is never so ascendant or successful that resurrection—the transcendence of death and the restoration of life—is either irrelevant or precluded. If everything is providential, then the issue in living is the patience and ingenuity of God's grace, and men need never live bereft of hope.

Yet, if providence is not luck or coincidence or mechanical guidance or a form of fatalism or an occasional special event, and, if providence is, so to speak, the historicity of grace, that does not dispel the mystery of the relationship of knowledge and time implicit in the idea of providence. And if, as I am suggesting, though everything be providential, our discernment is impaired or immature so that only certain happenings are identified as providential while others are ignored, that myopia or blindness to our own history is, I think, chiefly caused by our difficulties in comprehending the connection between knowledge and time. When, therefore, you or I call something providential, we are really saying that, in some sense, we have pierced the mystery of that dialectic; we have, somehow, glimpsed how knowledge and time are related.

Knowledge and time are differently related for men than for God, and in that difference is hidden the meaning of death as a moral power. Whatever knowledge—of anything whatever—men have is confined to time: we remember, we anticipate; we inherit knowledge, we transmit knowledge; we know this or that here and now—all of our knowledge is defined temporally. That is quite the same as recognizing that all human knowledge is fallen: the temporal limits of what men know are an aspect of the broken or disoriented or alienated actuality of fallen creation. The Fall is not, as the biblical literalists have supposed, an event in time, the Fall is the era of time as such—the Fall is the time of time, as it were. Human knowledge is temporal, fallen, and, as Saint Paul emphasizes, in bondage to death. Time is the realm of death. To say that our knowledge is temporal is to realize that we die and our knowledge is subjected to death. Death is a reality only in time; indeed, death is the essential reality of time.

Now the knowledge of God has more grandeur and is not imprisoned in time, which means His knowledge is whole, has no limits, is not defined by time. In biblical belief, however, God's knowledge, free of time, eternal, everlasting, enters time and is communicated, insofar as men may apprehend it, in time. Beyond the recognition of this extraordinary contrast between human knowledge and God's knowledge, there is little else which can be sensibly said (as far as I can discern) except that providence is a juncture in time between the partial and transient knowledge of men and the utter and transcendent knowledge of God.

Hence I was content to go along with Giselle's designation of my initial encounter with Dr. Porter as providential, having, as I have said, no more suitable description for it. What claimed my attention most, in thinking of this event as a matter of providence, was the retrospective side of it. What to me seemed most significant, if I regarded becoming Dr. Porter's patient as providential, was not what this augured for the future so much as what it recalled of the past. The most prominent feature of this providential happening—for me— was not anticipatory, but recollective, not foretelling, but remembering, not premonitive, but commemorative.

hails and farewells

That the surgeon and I had been contemporaries in East Harlem earlier in our lives was, somehow, a symbol of an experience of much greater scope that I was undergoing in the weeks immediately prior to the surgery. The clichés associated with impending death tell of the instantaneous recall of the dying person's life. Well, it *was* something like that, save that the recall I suffered of my own biography was not in an instant. It was, rather, episodic, occurring with more or less consciousness, and with more or less clarity, now and then, over a period of some weeks. I could not fix the dates (any more than I could fix the date of my beginning as a person—would it be the date of my birth certificate? or a date about nine months before? or, much further back, whenever there first was a man named Stringfellow? or, for that matter, the date of my baptism? or, whenever it may be said to be, when I became a Christian?). I do not really think it important to fix the dates. It was sometime before the operation and, then, continuing for some while after that. The matter of providence involving the surgeon was an especially prominent episode, but it was not the only one.

Bengt and Anthony were both strenuously opposed to any venture off the Island until the day came to enter the hospital, urging me, in accordance with common sense, to husband my waning energies as much and as long as possible. Rationally I concurred, and most of the commitments I had optimistically made, when there was hope that the therapy might succeed, were canceled.

The necessity, as it is ordinarily considered, of earning some income, despite the long period in which my earning capability had been so frequently interrupted and very drastically curtailed and regardless of the amount and complexity of my indebtedness, for medical care and for subsistence, was not an influential consideration at this point. I was so broke already, and my prospective debts for hospital, surgery and, if I survived, an indeterminate convalescence and uncertain capacity for work were such that a little more made little difference. My financial problems had not so much to do with the total sum of indebtedness as it had to do with the management of the debts, however much they were. In spite of my inherited Yankee attitudes, for which I retained a strong sentimental attachment, the economic realities which accompanied the illness were converting

me into classical Keynesian, upholding a doctrine of the viability of indefinite indebtedness.
I observed, somewhat ruefully, that my access
to credit had not been at all impaired, though
my income had been and though my future income prospects were bleak. But then, as I had
learned at firsthand while living in East Harlem,
in all of these matters of credit, cash and debts,
it makes a great difference, usually a decisive
difference, if one is a white, Anglo-Saxon American, preferably with a Harvard law degree. I
felt at the time, and I still harbor, a vehement
resentment against this society about all this:
bluntly, it is moral certainty that I would today
be dead if I were not a white, Anglo-Saxon,
with that preferred degree, because I would not
have been able—if I were black or an Indian
or a Chicano—to obtain credit sufficient to sur-
vive long enough to even determine the appropriate possible remedy for my condition. At
best, I would have died in some outpatient
clinic, awaiting a cursory diagnosis from an in-
experienced and harassed intern. Anyway, for
me, the matters of income and debt had been,
for the time being, put aside, and were of little
consequence in how the days were spent before November 22.

Though economics were irrelevant, the concern and counsel of Anthony and Bengt were
not. I nevertheless vetoed their edicts against
leaving the Island. I am not sure why: call it
a compulsion. I had a few places I wanted to

go; there were a few people I wanted to see; I
had a few things I wanted to say. My experience of the providential was not so much
premonitive as commemorative, even nostalgic.
I had no self-conscious premonition of death,
though I could, literally, feel death at work in
my body—indeed, I could see that in the mir-
ror; I had no pronounced fright of death, the
crisis about that had been met during the
months of pain and it had been resolved when
I was enabled to understand pain as work, as
I have already explained. I had the strongest
urge, however, to visit my own past. There
were some rituals required. It was necessary,
or at least it seemed important, without wholly
discerning why, to behold and accept and
salute my own past. So I would venture, before
the operation, a visit or two to America, as the
Islanders call the mainland; they were not sentimental journeys, yet they were not compelled
by any practical demands; they were, in my
intelligence, a way, symbolically, of verifying
the fact that I had finally been reconciled with
my own history as a person. And they were,
thus, confessional acts—gestures of repentance
(not regret or remorse, but repentance). And
they were, moreover, eucharistic acts—gestures
of thanksgiving for the grace that I had suffered
and enjoyed in the living of my life up to that
moment.

a political trial

A novel and extraordinary energy, inexplicable in terms of my emaciation, sustained me in going, for instance, to Baltimore, the situs of the trial of the "Catonsville Nine" accused by the State of conspiracy to obstruct the administration of the draft. The defendants, to notarize their opposition to the slaughter in Vietnam and their apprehension about the militarization of American society, had concocted a batch of napalm, using an Army-training-manual recipe, which they used to destroy selective service files at a draft board office in Catonsville, Maryland. Two of the nine on trial were and are particular friends of mine—the Berrigan brothers, Philip, a Josephite priest, and Daniel, a Jesuit. A good many other citizens—lots of whom I knew from other causes and struggles—had assembled in Baltimore in visible and vocal support of the accused and of the protest which the defendants represented against American barbarism. At the courthouse and at a church where they assembled each evening during the trial, these

citizens were, literally, surrounded by hundreds
of Federal agents and double agents and mar-
shals and police turned out and deployed as
troops, weapons at the ready. It was, superfi-
cially, a startling sight, reminiscent of a Nazi
newsreel, but that was an impression which only
survived until one remembered that the Federal surveillance of citizens is now as routine
as it is ubiquitous, that the FBI ignores the
First Amendment practically as a matter of policy, and that it was nearly a decade ago that
the transmutation of the police into a military
organization began and that it is now virtually
complete. That the Baltimore scene during the
trial of the Catonsville Nine seemed a carica-
ture of Nazism, say, of the vintage of 1936, intrigued the mind only until one focused on the
fact that this was but one of several patently
political prosecutions which the State had lately
used for the purpose of intimidating dissenters.
Because I have fully supported such protest
ever since I became enlightened about the
wickedness and stupidity of this war during the
visit I made to Vietnam in early 1966, I take
nothing away from the dignity and necessity
of the anti-war protest, in this trial as well as
otherwise, if I mention that other issues besides
the war are involved, profoundly, in the Berrigan trial and similar political proceedings, notably including those against the Black Panthers.
In fact the survival of due process of law—

which is, of course, the hallmark distinguishing
a free society from totalitarianism—is at stake.
How long can the public authorities—the police,
the investigative and intelligence agencies, the
public prosecutors, and, alas, sometimes, the
judges abuse, circumvent or subvert due process
before it is effectually destroyed both as an idea
and as an institution? And so I was brought to
Baltimore, brought there by my past, by the
conjunction, there, of many issues and the congregation of many persons with which I had
been engaged before: the protest against the
war, and the very survival in this society of
dissent as such; the friendship of the Berrigan
brothers, and my esteem for their Christianity,
and my admiration for their guts; the assault
instigated by the State against the only thing
in which citizens have safety from the State—
due process of law, and the pathetic struggle
to save due process; the embodiment in so
many of the others in Baltimore that day of
other involvements now, somehow, summed up
in the gathering at the trial.

In the evening I went, with Anthony, who
had been there with Bishop Pike since the open-
ing of the trial, and with Rafael Martinez, a
friend of many years and in many battles in
New York, to the church where everyone was
to congregate. The attitude of the ecclesiastical
authorities toward the defendants had been
made emphatic, a day or two earlier, in a statement to the press of the Archbishop of Balti-

more, within whose jurisdiction the protest had been made, which was reported to say that he "washed his hands" of the clergy and others who had accomplished the witness. Hearing of this, I had tried to reassure the Berrigan brothers: "Cheer up," I told them, "maybe this shows that the Archbishop has been reading the Bible."

The congregation—I suppose, technically, it was a paracongregation—which that night assembled, save for the numerous and ludicrously obvious government agents who had been assigned to infiltrate and spy upon the happening, in poignant contrast to the disclaimer of the chief priest, acclaimed the accused. I suspect the spies present thought the event political and very radical at that. Radical it was: one of the more radical liturgies in which I have ever participated. And political, too, but in the elementary eschatological sense that all biblically authentic liturgy is political, not in the corny ideological simplistics in which the FBI construes politics.

I was exhausted, but this scene was exhilarating. The pain was unspeakably severe and had not been appeased by any medicine, but, amidst this congregation, it was not debilitating. I could walk only with extreme effort, but I was not enfeebled. Dan Berrigan asked if I would speak. I said that I would just greet everyone. When I stood before them and the words came out, however, they were not a salutation. The words were a benediction:

Remember, now, that the State has only one power it can use against human beings: death. The State can persecute you, prosecute you, imprison you, exile you, execute you. All of these mean the same thing. The State can consign you to death. The grace of Jesus Christ in this life is that death fails. There is nothing the State can do to you, or to me, which we need fear.

There was some silence. Then there was an ovation, which took me by surprise, until Anthony pointed out that it was the failure of death that the people applauded. Then, spontaneously, the congregation sang.

a black ghetto

My will to accept my own past had been en-
acted on another scene, a few days before the
visit in Baltimore with the congregation of the
Catonsville Nine. I had been at the colleges in
Jackson, Tennessee, in the hinterland between
Nashville and Memphis. It is ostentatious Wallace country. The 1968 presidential campaign
was then underway, and canvas banners pro-
claiming "You are now entering Wallace country!" were stretched across the principal en-
trance highways to the town. There are two
colleges in Jackson, one black—Lane College,
and one white—Lambuth College, both of them
church-related. The two schools have begun to
collaborate some, and my invitation had been
to give lectures on each campus, but, in each
case, under the joint auspices of both colleges
and before audiences from both.

Just as it is *everywhere,* Jackson, Tennessee,
has its black ghetto—a squalid shantytown, adjacent to a dump, through which the rail freight
lines run, a dozen or so muddy streets lined

with decrepit tar-paper shacks, without plumb-
ing indoors or a sewage system underground,
without safe or reliable utilities—where there is
any heat or light at all, without sidewalks or
streetlights or traffic controls, without recrea-
tional facilities for young or old—unless a pol-
luted creek be counted, without public trans-
portation and, therefore, ready access to jobs
and to the rest of the community—if that be a
term applicable to Jackson's white-bourgeois
ghetto. Lately the citizens of Fite's Bottom, as
the black ghetto is known, had been organizing
themselves to deal with their problems as tenants, with their needs in education and employment, and there had even been talk of register-
ing to vote. There was, as you can see, black
militancy a-borning in Fite's Bottom, and the
local white establishment was already working
up an hysteria—and schemes of repression—to
cope with what they deemed, in their pathology, an alien, revolutionary threat. (Militancy,
indeed! How can it be called militant, in America, for citizens to seek the redemption of a con-
stitutional ethic which is two centuries old?)
Some of the good citizens of Fite's Bottom had
heard that I would be in Jackson and I was
invited to visit them and see this place. I had
seen the place before. On three thousand days
in East Harlem I had seen this same place three
thousand times. And I had seen it in the other
Jackson, in Mississippi, while working on some
of the Freedom Ride cases. I had seen it, too,

in an aboriginal slum in Perth, Australia. Spiro
Agnew is really quite correct: when you have
seen one black shantytown or slum, you've seen
them all. What has often intrigued me, having
seen them all, is the essential difference there
must be between a man, like myself, who is free
to see other places and the person, like one of
those from Fite's Bottom, who sees no other
place. Beyond that most basic difference, which
is inherent in the American ghettoization, and
which no white man—however discerning or
compassionate or, for that matter, however deprived or poor—can ever breach, is an astonishment I have much felt that so many whites
have never seen any black ghettos. It is an almost incomprehensible blindness which afflicts
most American whites; they have not even seen
the images of the black ghettos that have literally occupied their television screens on the
daily newscasts for nearly a decade and a half.
And they have not turned the corners or
glanced away from their highways or crossed
the tracks to see the black ghetto adjacent to
their own lily-white ghetto. And so they do not
even know that *they* are ghettoized, they do
not realize that they are captives, and, hence,
can they exist in profound moral confusion, en-
tertaining their own captivity as if it were their
freedom.

That is the way it was in Jackson when I went
there. Hardly anyone in the white society there
knew anything of significance about Fite's Bot-

tom. Oh, the whites knew vaguely that Jackson had a bottom, and they either agreed or went along with the custom which sanctioned the bottom as the place for the blacks. But only the fewest whites, including those from the white college, had ever gone further than that or ever bothered to see the place or ever cared to do so.

Still, if Jackson's white folk were, on the whole, depressing to be among, I found people in Fite's Bottom refreshing to be with. I had had that experience before, too. There is a specific veracity to the resurrection in the black ghettos of America. That life survives at all in such circumstances is impressive; that life so often prevails there, practically speaking, proves the grace of God, by showing the triumph of life in the midst of death. The spirit of the resurrection is loose in the black ghettos. Sometimes it is called "Soul." It is the humanizing spirit. It is, as I knew, again, in Fite's Bottom, mercifully, contagious.

The main responsibility I had for the colleges was to be, one evening, a theological critic of the two local candidates for Congress, one John T. Williams, a Republican, and the incumbent, Representative Ray Blanton, a registered Democrat and covert (though not very) Wallaceite. The two of them were to debate and I was to comment on the theological implications of their views. A considerable crowd, from both colleges and from both ghettos, assembled. I

gathered that the event was historic in one regard: it was the first time any citizens from
Fite's Bottom had ever attended a public meeting concerning politics. Mr. Williams failed to
materialize, and no wonder, a Republican was
an anomaly in this district, though it must be
noticed that this took place before the Nixon-
Agnew-Mitchell strategy to procure the Wallace
movement had become so open, and so successful. The Congressman spoke "at length on the
power of the Russian and American nuclear
arsenals," as a newspaper reported it, and "de-
cried Federal control of public schools and
urged the maintenance of locally directed law
enforcement. 'Local control' he said, means
local responsiveness to local conditions." Having been in Fite's Bottom that very day, I mentioned that I had difficulty, in listening to
Representative Blanton, comprehending how
he could speak as he did and ignore utterly the
scandal of Fite's Bottom. It is, I believe, and
I said that night, a familiar insight of biblical
theology, much stressed by Saint Paul, later
taken up by Saint Augustine, nearer our day
upheld by Dietrich Bonhoeffer or, in this country, honored by Reinhold Niebuhr, that moral
responsibility is verified as relevant and *bona
fide* where concern is joined with the capability
of action. It becomes, in other words, nonsensical and morally decadent to discuss Soviet mis-
siles, as to which even a Congressman from
Tennessee has, at most, a remote influence, if

at the same time "local conditions" are rationalized or ignored by those, like a Congressman,
who possess some effectual power for change.
Theologically, I was, I trust, quite orthodox,
though I was not abstract about it. Midway in
my remarks, just as I began to document, from
my recent observation, the "local conditions,"
the Congressman, his complexion livid, rose,
gathered his script, summoned his attachés,
and stalked, rather noisily, as it seemed to me,
from the auditorium. The delegation from
Fite's Bottom rejoiced, also rather noisily. Some
students from both colleges joined them. There
was a general tumult. I seemed to me to be the
only calm person there, but then, I was more
or less numb from my disease anyway. After a
while, I resumed my theological discourse and,
after that, there was a long and, most of all, an
open discussion among the people of Jackson,
white and black.

Now and then I receive news from Fite's Bottom. The Congressman was re-elected, needless
to mention, but not without a pledge to himself
to visit the place (I hope he had the foresight
to wear rubbers) and do *something*. And then
on New Year's Eve, 1968, a fire swept through
the shantytown. I am told that many students,
from both colleges, volunteered their labor and
money, clothing and household items to help in
the emergency. I heard this news as an omen—
of hope—for Fite's Bottom needed to be destroyed: all the black ghettos need to burn, and

all that talk of renovating the slums of America is actually contrived to evade the truth, for white and black alike, that if there is to be any hope, the ghettos must be destroyed.

an ecclesiastical event

My return, as it were, to my past, to persons
and issues with which I had expended so much
of my life, symbolized by the situation of Fite's
Bottom and the trial at Baltimore, was more
arduous when I went to Kansas City, Missouri,
to address the national convention of the Disciples of Christ denomination. I recall intro-
specting some about it, at the time, and, in
retrospect, too, I see it as a token of my own
ecclesiastical involvement. That had been, as I
have noted, precocious and extensive. Having
renounced the priesthood and any other sort
of churchly occupation, I gradually found myself in extraordinary demand as a preacher and
speaker and consultant and teacher and leader
in blatantly churchy circles. This was already
an issue for me while I was a student, but it
was intensified as the years passed, greatly so
by my decision to work in East Harlem and
then, later on, when I began to write. It would,
perhaps, not have been a problem if, in the in-
terim between adolescence and adulthood, I

had not become a confessing Christian. It would have been alright, I think, if I had managed to remain steadfast as a nominal Christian or a churchman. Instead I had been converted, if that word can here be used without its corny and profane connotations. I forbear describing *that* ordeal, for now, except to say that, along the way, I had entered into the reading of the Bible—a bizarre thing for an Episcopalian to do, I know, and a traumatic exploit for anybody. There is, simply, this danger in reading the Bible that one may be emancipated from the jargon, stereotypes, fables and similar encumbrances of church tradition and hear the Word of God. Well, I was being (I am being) regularly devastated in the privacy of my encounter with the biblical Word and that kept challenging the propriety of my ecclesiastical activities.

Too much of the immense resources of American Christendom, in the National Council of Churches and in the established denominations, were engaged in playing church in endless and revolving conferences and training sessions and consultations. The whole verbose, redundant enterprise was becoming so dissipated in talking about the Christian witness in society that few energies were leftover to *do* the witness, assuming—which is something which conscience generally precluded—that the talk was responsible or even sensible. On this scene, as I saw it, I had become something of a curiosity—a layman who was a Christian, a non-professional who could be theologically articulate. In the confidence of our friendship, Anthony and I used to joke about "William Stringfellow, the boy theologian." Others bestowed different titles, probably the most frequent reference, publicly, to my "role" was as that of "gadfly." What was meant, I guess, was that, having no vested interest in the ecclesiastical establishment (aha! except, perchance, the gadfly role!), I was free, and otherwise competent, enough to complain and criticize, prod and plead about the churches in contemporary America. Too often the difficulty with that task, I found, was that the ecclesiastical authorities, bureaucrats, and flunkies whom I addressed actually relished criticism as a means of further avoiding reformation or renewal. They were flagellants, morbidly enjoying punishment for misbehavior in which they fully intended to persevere. My involvement as "gadfly" or whatever-you-call-it was becoming a charade.

I would drop out of it. And I did, although, in the case of my own denomination, it would be more accurate to say that, before I had a chance to drop out, I was rejected by the ecclesiastical establishment of the Episcopal Church. There were intimations of that in several situations where invitations for my participation in this or that churchly event were issued and then withdrawn. There had been a proposal to censure me at a General Convention of the Church. I was informed that some Episcopal seminaries had found me to be "too controversial" to have as a visiting lecturer. The bishops of some dioceses specifically asked me not to appear in parishes within their jurisdictions; one wrote that my coming to his diocese would be "premature." These things came to some sort of culmination, of course, when Bishop Pike asked that I be his legal counsel in the heresy proceedings that had been instituted against him, and when Anthony and I wrote and published the book about that conflict, *The Bishop Pike Affair*. It is, I most earnestly affirm, a responsible, scrupulously truthful book. Anthony and I had felt somewhat flattered when we learned that a Madison Avenue-type public relations man had been engaged to try to prevent the book from being reviewed on certain television programs and the like. With such enemies, we were sure, for once, we had done something right. Months later, while I was preoccupied in illness, news came of another reprisal because of that book: I had been removed from the Faith and Order Commission of the World Council of Churches, where, for six years, I had represented the Episcopal Church, and where I had been the only layman and one of but a handful of persons under forty years of age. To this day I have never been informed officially about this by the elders of the Church; the word first reached me from an English newspaper that lamented the deed, later letters from many colleagues on the commission filled in the details. There is a comity in the World Council of Churches, not dissimilar to senatorial courtesy, which dictates that an appointee to a council body be acceptable to the authorities of his own church. In effect, and despite protests from representatives of other churches in Africa, Asia, and both Western and Eastern Europe, I was removed because I was (I suppose I still am) personally obnoxious to the Episcopalian authorities. Ironically, of all of my churchly involvements, Faith and Order had been the one which was, though the commission be cumbersome and slow and conservative, worthwhile. Faith and Order is ponderous and, perhaps, too self-serious, but it is not a dishonest enterprise, and it is not a facetious effort, and it was these latter regions in Christendom that I had determined to quit.

I lay for a long time on a hotel bed in Kansas City attended by such reminiscences. In another hour or two I was to address this church convention. *What the hell am I doing here?* I thought. *This is not the Church: this is some American aberration of the Church.* I either cursed or prayed, the two being hard to distinguish. I read Ephesians. Unlike some friends of my own generation—like Harvey Cox or Malcolm Boyd—I do not denigrate institutionalism as such in the Church. I see, specifically in the account of Pentecost, that the Church's peculiar vocation is as an institution—as the exemplary principality—as the holy nation. So

147

ideas of a non-institutional church or a deinstitutionalized church or underinstitutionalized church seem to me to be as nebulous as the Greek philosophy from which such ideas come and contrary to the biblical precedent. That does not temper my critique of the inherited churchly institutions; in fact it sharpens it and makes it more urgent. Now that mark which verifies the integrity of the Church as institution and sets the Church apart from the other institutions—the State, the university, the Pentagon, General Electric, *et al*—as the exemplary or pioneer or holy institution is the freedom of the Church from primary and controlling concern about her own survival. Survival of the institution is the operative ethic of all institutions, *in their fallenness*. The Church is called into being in freedom from that ethic of survival and where renewal or reformation in the Church happens for real, that very freedom is being exercised, and the Church is viable and faithful. *It's all there, in Ephesians*, I smiled, *my speech is in Ephesians*. And so it was.

an apostolic succession?

It was no novelty for me to prepare for a public address through reading the Bible, as I did for the Disciples assembled in Kansas City. I have no particular procedure about this, it has just become a natural thing to do. It is premeditated negatively, however, in that there are some resorts to the biblical material that I do not, and that I will not, make. I do not, having an opinion already in mind, search and scrounge in Scripture for a proof-text. And, furthermore, I do not believe that, despite whatever other sense God can be said to furnish guidance to men, God is so picayunish that He inspires preachers or others who speak to locate specific texts which He has picked out beforehand. These represent abuses of the Bible, common though they may be. In fact it is exactly such familiar manipulations of the Bible that cause men to mistakenly think that the Bible is trite and archaic. Quite apart from the issue of belief, there is no intrinsic reason why any contemporary man could regard the Bible as irrelevant.

He might find it unagreeable, threatening, provocative, but not irrelevant. It is the gross misrepresentation of the character of the biblical witness as such, illustrated by the false uses to which the Bible is so much subjected by professed believers, like those mentioned, that occasions the indifference of many to the relevancy and contemporaneity of the biblical Word.

To rely, in preparation for and in delivery of a public utterance, upon the Bible requires an esteem for the integrity of the Bible as a living Word, which men can hear and communicate and discuss, rather than a treatment of the Bible as if it were some dead words which the preacher undertakes to resuscitate. That esteem for the Bible comes out of a continuing experience with the Bible, a common life with the Bible, a personal immersion in the biblical story, a graphic identification with—really, *in*—the biblical drama, a recurring encounter with the Word, a confessional relationship with the living Word. In this context, my Kansas City conduct for that speech was merely a normal thing.

Besides, I have never had a theology of my own, or a theology adapted from anybody else, to commend to others. Even as a "boy theologian"—an appellative which has fallen into disuse in the household ever since Martin Marty called me "Protestantism's angry middle-aged man"—I did not have my own theology. I trust

I never shall. Moreover, I could not be thought theologically learned, having never studied theology academically. Still, I am sometimes aware that people—especially fellow laymen—assume that I have read prodigiously in theology, whereas the truth is that I am practically a theological illiterate, so far as the works of the theologians are concerned. In my whole life I have, maybe, read two dozen theological books, Aquinas or Calvin or Tillich or the like. (If I boast, I boast of my weakness.) The truth is I have, practically, just read the Bible.

Because of his pointed remarks to me during the public dialogue with Karl Barth, at the University of Chicago, during Barth's American visit in 1962, and his generous reference in *Evangelical Theology,* I know that many suppose that most of the theological books I have read are books of Karl Barth. The truth is only three are, although, as one might expect, I entertain an intention eventually to read all of Barth. (Also, all of Augustine, all of Luther, all of Bonhoeffer—I am not so sure I will read any more than I have of Aquinas, Calvin and Tillich.) I am, hence, usually amused when I hear myself being accused (it always sounds like an accusation) of being a "Barthian."

More seriously, I raised with Karl Barth during his visit the matter which is basic here. Again and again, in both the public dialogue and in our private conversations, it had been my experience that as Barth began to make

some point, I would at once know what he was
going to say. It was not some intuitive thing,
it differed from that, it was a recognition, in
my mind, of something familiar that Barth was
articulating. When this had happened a great
many times while I listened to him, I described
my experience to him and asked why this would
happen. His response was instantaneous: "How
could it be otherwise? We read the same Bible,
don't we?"

To think and speak and act with a decent
respect for the independence and efficacy of the
Word of God, in the Bible and in the world,
is, as Barth so well exemplified among the theological professionals and among the prisoners
to whom he regularly preached in the Basel jail,
the substance of Christian practice. It is a practice which can (even) be heard and (now and
then) be heeded in the ecclesiastical councils,
for all their vanity and motion. Anyway, with
such conviction I had done my thing in Kansas
City.

The next morning I had breakfast with Josh
Wilson, a Disciples of Christ minister in the
California-Nevada jurisdiction of that denomination. Josh, in terms of his function and office
in that tradition, was equivalent to a bishop in
churches of the Episcopal system. He has been
deeply implicated in experimental ministries,
particularly open to new forms of congrega-
tional life, and is a friend of mine of long
standing, ever since I had first become ac-

quainted with him and with his witness, during a visit some years before to some of the congregations under his care. It is a comfort—and a fact which ameliorates the pedantry and solemnity of churchly conventions—that these assemblies inadvertently, as it were, cause numbers of Christians, otherwise scattered about, to meet one another and from that a network of the concerned within many denominations and amongst many churches has emerged in the country. If anyone attending a churchy meeting suffers frustration over the discrepancies between the proceedings and Christian practice, he can take heart that there are commonly others present who share the same sentiment, and, at the least, their contact in the situation may create a community of protest on the scene itself or furnish a mutual interest and support when they disperse. I suppose this is an inconvenient way for Christians to find each other, but it *is* one way, and, through the multiversity of ecumenical, interdenominational, sectarian and other assorted ecclesiastical conclaves in, say, the past two decades, a clandestine, more or less extemporaneous, yet definite community —transcending virtually all the inherited churchly separations—has gained vitality and significance. If God is patient enough to allow renewal of the Church to originate from within the churches—a moot matter if the experience of the old ecclesiastical establishment, Israel, is recognized, according to the *New* Testament—

it is, I do believe, from this hidden company
within the churches that it will come.

Without formalities, Josh Wilson and I
shared this peculiar covenant, with hosts of
others, in spite of time and distances, which
made our actual encounters only occasional
and, then, usually on the alien territory of some
ecclesiastical convention. We talked some at
breakfast about the meeting and heard news
from each other about others of the covenant,
but, by this stage in the disease, my appearance
had become ghastly: my complexion blanched,
my eyes sunken and dulled, my body—never
imposing—diminished extremely, thus, the conversation turned to the crisis in my health. Josh
wondered what this meant vocationally, and
whether, if I lived for any appreciable time
longer, the tasks which I had had would change.
I had not examined that at all, as yet; I had
not anticipated anything beyond the surgery. In
truth, I had never dwelt elaborately upon vocationally rationalizing what I had been doing.
I practiced law—some colleagues of that profession had thought it eccentric when, in 1956,
I moved to East Harlem to begin my practice,
but, within a decade after that, attitudes in the
law schools and in the profession had changed
enough so that what I had done was no longer
considered so odd. I spoke—perhaps I talked too
much in speeches, but I hoped that, more often
than not, this was an act of rogation (as at Kansas City) and/or a gift of advocacy (as with

the cause of Fite's Bottom) and/or a pastoral effort (as in the Baltimore trial). I wrote books —though I thought of this as derivative and subsidiary and I frequently felt surprise when someone called me an author: I wrote and published, paradoxically, come to think of it, mainly as a private exercise by which to liberate my being from this or that concern so that I could go on to something else. I told Josh that, at this juncture, it didn't matter much what I had done or whether sense could be made of it vocationally, and, as to where I might find myself vocationally after the operation, speculation was not very edifying—I might find myself in hell!

Wilson saw more coherence in my past vocationally than I had noticed myself. The itinerant public speaker part of it he conceived as an ambassadorship by which those visited and addressed in a particular place are tangibly assured of the existence of other persons and other communities of complimentary commitment elsewhere. Elements of advocacy—having a free voice to use for others' causes, of the pastoral—being available and vulnerable to listen to others, of apologetics—especially upholding the biblical tradition of the Church to expose the apostasy of the churches, of service —that is, living in the world as a servant of the world, he thought, correlated in the emissary function. "You really are a bishop, Bill," Josh announced flatly, "a roving bishop."

This casual consecration startled me. I had

not vocationally rationalized my doings very much at all, as I have mentioned; I certainly hadn't entered the realm of Josh Wilson's reasoning. I looked at him squarely. He was not facetious. "It takes one to know one," I told him, thinking of the Apostolic succession.

IV HOPE

Many one there be that say of my soul, There is no help for him in his God.

But thou, O Lord, art my defender; thou art my worship, and the lifter up of my head.

I did call upon the Lord with my voice, and he heard me out of his holy hill.

I laid me down and slept, and rose up again; for the Lord sustained me.

Psalm 3:2–5

The days next before November 22, I had in virtual solitude. I was to be admitted to the Columbia-Presbyterian Hospital the evening of the twentieth for examinations and tests preliminary to the surgery. I had left the Island early the day before that and spent the interval in the city with myself.

Anthony would follow me to New York so as to be able to visit the hospital the day before the operation, and he had announced that he intended to wait at the hospital during the event. Stuart Wetmore, the Suffragan Bishop of New York, an old friend whom I esteemed as a man and respected as a priest and bishop, would also come the afternoon before to celebrate the Holy Communion. Dan Berrigan, now free on bond pending appeal of his conviction, called to say that he had obtained judicial permission to come to the city to see me, and so I had suggested he join the Eucharist.

I had seen my father and mother in Northampton, as I have earlier said, and I had

thanked most of our Block Island neighbors.
Since the immigration to the Island, I had been
ill and unable to participate much in Island life,
except to go occasionally to one of the Island
congregations, the First Baptist Church or St.
Andrew's Roman Catholic Church, and except
for the time the principal, aware that I had
known Martin Luther King Jr., invited me to
speak at a memorial program the school held
after Dr. King's assassination. The Island resi-
dents had been, consistent with a Yankee
ethos, discreet—that is, they minded their own
business—and yet, they had been at the same
time ready and generous in their welcome. The
arts of phoniness are, on the whole, not practiced on Block Island. Both Anthony and I have
come to regard this place as home and felt acceptance in the community: we could be con-
fident we had neighbors reliable in need. I had
been specifically conscious of a concern among
our Island friends about my health. Later on,
after I returned from the hospital, Bengt had
confided that the consensus among them all had
been an apprehension of my death. I had not
been expected back. On that November morning, however, when I departed for the hospital,
I realized that Block Island was the place to
which I would like to return to live.

absolution

The writing of the manuscript of the study-book for the Confraternity of Christian Doctrine, *Imposters of God,* had suffered from repeated interruption and prolonged inattention, during the course of the disease. Mary Perkins Ryan, the editor of the series of which this was to be one volume, had been patient and considerate each time the completion of the book had been delayed, and I felt keenly about finishing it not only because Mary had so long awaited it, and not because I was satisfied with the manuscript or thought it so worthy as prose, but also because it had been the only thing that I would call work, in a strict or narrow sense, which I had been engaged in within about a year. It had been terribly difficult, with the distraction of the pain and my fatigue from *that* work, to persevere in writing even this modest paperback. The manuscript would lie on my desk for days and days when I would be unable to touch it, unable to bear sitting at the desk, indeed, to review what had been done much less succeed in concentrating on proceeding with it. I had a vague conviction, however, that I had to work on it whenever I could do so, and, on days scattered through the spring and summer of 1968, when my tolerance of my distress was strong, I had returned to the manuscript.

I brought *Imposters* with me when I left the Island for the hospital; it was, now, at last, close to being done. I rose very early on the morning of the day I was to enter the hospital, consumed some coffee, and read what had been written. I was not satisfied, but, then, I have never written anything that I can recall with which I have been wholly satisfied. (That is an odd fact about writing—when you compose something and commit to paper, the illusion is that you have, so to speak, materialized a thought, perfected an idea, reached a conclusion. The illusion is that there has been a creation sufficient to record. Actually, in my experience, it is the other way around: to write something is to expose its partiality, its tentativeness, its transience. In that sense, I have never been satisfied with my own writing.) I was not satisfied with *Imposters*, but, to my surprise, it had a coherence. I found that I could concentrate well on this morning, and, curiously, of all days, on this day I felt no pain. By noon, the manuscript was done—as much so as it would ever be—and I put it in the mail to Mary Ryan.

My nostalgic ventures, the ritual visitations
to my own past, these episodes of symbolic recall, these vivid excursions which, somehow,
breached time and compressed time, so that all
reality of which I knew was in the present moment and to speak of past, or of future, for that
matter, was quite arbitrary, were enough now.
Whether I would ever suffer similar experience
again was a question that did not occur to me,
although, as I have intimated, there was such
in the aftermath of the surgery. More accurately, in hindsight, the operation itself was one
of these peculiar episodes—the climactic one.
But, on this day, as I packed a suitcase for the
hospital, I knew that there had been enough—
enough to understand what had been happening.

These were not forlorn journeys, indulgent
reminiscences, sentimental exercises—they were
not nostalgic in any of these connotations. My
compulsion to go to some places, my need to
commemorate certain facets of the past, my recall experience as a whole was a nostalgia which
expressed an eschatological hope. This was a
way I had been coming to terms with my own
existence confessionally—a mode, indeed, of repentance—a means of my acceptance of myself,
of my life in its totality, of both the furthest
outreaches and the most secret parts of my life,
of the meaning of my own life, *whatever* that
be.

Nostalgia means hope, I thought. I had shut

the suitcase, and I stretched out on the bed to consider this more. I noticed that I still didn't hurt. It was now midafternoon, I had worked the morning on *Imposters*, done my packing chore, was ready to check out of the hotel and check into the hospital: I had not yet felt pain this day. *That's strange*, I mumbled audibly. *Nostalgia is hope*, I said that out loud, returning to my first thought.

It seemed a contradictory notion, but as I lay there, feeling good, repeating the idea in my mind, the contradiction eluded me, for I had recognized a dozen different—quite different—situations in which nostalgia is hope. One of those, which remains prominent today because it continues with a vengeance sanctioned by the awful power of incumbency, is how the inherited racism and pathetic anxiety for moral justification of the white middle classes, the famous majority to which silence is imputed, had been exploited in John Mitchell's management of the Nixon presidential campaign which had lately succeeded electorally. The cultivation of the white backlash in "middle America"—as the euphemists have styled it—is an appeal for the restoration of the ethics and virtues of an American past that symbolizes and, supposedly, once approximated paradise. *The nostalgia is eschatological!* That the image of this idyllic American past is legendary, rather than historically accurate, is irrelevant to the potency of this appeal. In fact, it is the imperfected and

tarnished historical actuality—a nineteenth-
century America of Victorian pietism, religious
persecution, colonialism and foreign conquest,
chauvinism, the sanctification of property
rights, and ascendant white supremacy—an
America governed by hypocrisy, bigotry, aggression, greed and violence—for which the
white majority yearns. That is *their* paradise,
and Mr. Nixon has learned to bespeak their
longing as if it were the most holy aspiration,
while the Attorney General has discovered it
can be harnessed in order to enlarge power.
That the nostalgic, in this example, is focused
upon a twisted version of the past or that the
eschatological vision is perverse did not seem
to me, as I lay there brooding over it, to diminish the force of the truism but to endorse it.

It seemed that I had meditated a long time,
though when I glanced at my watch I found
that it had been barely ten minutes. *Nostalgia
is hope,* I muttered, aloud, again, as I rose from
the bed. The reconciliation of a person with,
and within, his own history is the same issue
for a man as his reconciliation in future, escha-
tologically. Reconciliation, as a biblical reality,
breaches time, past and future; reconciliation
transcends time; reconciliation breaks out of the
bondage to the power of death, which time
makes tangible. Reconciliation defeats time.

I looked at the watch once more. It was *time*
to go to the hospital. I laughed about that. *I
had no time left: I had all the time in the world.*

an ecumenical sacrament

I had all the time there is; the time had come for the Eucharist. The first hospital night had passed without pain, though I had not taken medication which had been supplied. I slept soundly, though I had not used the sleeping tablets that were prescribed, having a prejudice against their use, which I attribute to my Yankee inheritance. Anthony had arrived in the city that evening and had come to Columbia-Presbyterian to see that I was settled. He had come bearing various messages and several gifts.

The featured present was a circus poster, which he hung in the room so that it would be a constant vision no matter how I might be positioned. He knew this would comfort and delight me, since I am a more than avid fan of the circus, regarding it as the auspices of the most sophisticated and versatile performing arts and counting the survival of the circus in America as a reliable gauge of the survival of civility itself. I am, of course, referring to the circus—

167

not to Disney productions, not to Ed Sullivan's facsimiles, not to the Broadway pretenses with which John Ringling North, as if renouncing his birthright, had adulterated the arena performances of "The Greatest Show on Earth"—where it retains integrity both as art and enterprise. In the summer of 1966, Anthony and I had spent nearly three months traveling with the Clyde Beatty-Cole Brothers Circus, the largest remaining tented show, in order to gather material and gain firsthand background for a book I purpose to write about the idea of society as a circus and, hence, the circus as an eschatological scene. Roughly half of that book had been written when I became enough impaired by the disease that it had to be put aside until a more opportune time. It was a gift which suited the circumstances entirely.

As if to multiply my pleasure, I opened one of the messages that Anthony brought to find a note from Corita Kent—who had become celebrated as Sister Corita of the Order of the Immaculate Heart of Mary for her serigraphs and whom I had asked to do the jacket for my circus book—together with one of her posters announcing an edition of her work under the legend (a citation from e. e. cummings) "damn everything but the circus."

During the next morning I had received telephone calls from Giselle Klopstock and the Rev. Melvin Schoonover. Giselle had indicated that she or Robert would visit sometime that day. Mel and I had been friends and colleagues since 1956 in East Harlem. He had been administrator of the East Harlem Protestant Parish, but had resigned from the group ministry, not long after I had done the same, and subsequently became minister of the Chambers Memorial Baptist Church in the same neighborhood. I had been his best man in his wedding and his daughter, Polly, was one of my godchildren, whom I regularly took to the circus, of course. Mel has been unable to walk since his birth and functions with impressive agility and virtual independence from his wheel chair. He knows more of illness and pain and, therefore, more about health and wholeness, than any other person within my experience. Though he is consistently cool about his own condition, I detected, in our conversation on the phone, that he was anxious about my condition, and I had sought to change the subject by asking his suggestions for a Christmas present for Polly.

Thomas Pike, a priest from the city, deeply involved through the Episcopal Peace Fellowship in the anti-war protests (recently he was arrested, with others, for praying on Pentagon premises), had also been in touch with me at the hospital, particularly to ask if I wished to receive the Holy Communion. Tom said he would be there to assist Bishop Wetmore.

Early in the afternoon, Anthony returned to

the hospital and he and I talked about the circus, as if to anticipate the Eucharist.

Soon Dan Berrigan joined us, then Mel Schoonover, Robert Klopstock, Tom Pike. By the arrival of the bishop, Ann Thompson and Merritt Hedgeman had also appeared. Ann Thompson is an earnest and gifted Christian whom Anthony and I had come to know when we shared a household in the city. She had been our housekeeper, and she had brought some order to our home, but, more than that, she is a radiant person, and she had brought some light there too. We had kept in touch with her after immigrating to the Island. Anthony had written to her about my situation. Together with his wife, Anna Arnold Hedgeman, an illustrious pioneer among black women in America, Merritt Hedgeman had been stanch counsel for years in the vicissitudes that I, as a white man, had to confront on the scene of the black revolt.

Those who had not met before were introduced by Anthony and, as that happened, it seemed to me that my biography was being recited, so truly did this congregation conjoin to represent many persons and many things that I had known and for which I cared. More important, it was a *good* congregation in which there were old and young, rich and poor, white and black; in which Anglicans, Baptists, Roman Catholics, Pentecostals, Methodists, and lapsed churchmen were present: in which some had education, but some not, some had known imprisonments, but some had not, some were of the establishment, but some not.

Bishop Wetmore declared the sacrament of Holy Communion is ecumenical and that everyone would be welcome to receive the bread and the wine. He asked Father Berrigan to read the Epistle. And so, together, thanksgiving for life was made to God.

Afterward, as people dispersed, Anthony escorted the bishop to the elevator. When he came back to the room, and after we were alone, he said that as they walked down the hall, Bishop Wetmore had remarked, with evident excitement: "What an extraordinary congregation that was! I wish they were all like that!"

vigil

Twenty-four hours later, when it had been thought that the operation would be over, the surgical team was still at work.

I had been anesthetized in the early morning of November 22 and removed from my hospital room. Anthony saw my departure. I have only groggy images of it, among them one of making a strenuous effort to tell Anthony something important as I was being taken away. He since informs me that the urgent message asked him to be certain to get a particular Christmas present, from me, for Polly. Dr. Porter had explained to me, lucidly, the procedure contemplated in surgery and he had mentioned various contingencies. If the event went reasonably well, he indicated it would be done in about three hours. If, of course, there were a calamity, it might be over in less time. Beyond such foresights, there were only incalculable uncertainties. Still, it appeared likely that there would be definite news by the afternoon.

The work began around ten in the morning. I had urged Anthony to spend this interval at a movie or at a bar, but he wished to wait at the hospital and he had undertaken to advise my father and mother of the outcome, as well as keep other persons, several of them scattered in distant parts of the country, posted by telephone. So Anthony began a vigil. During it, he was joined, from time to time, by many of those who had been members of the congregation of the day previous, and, toward the end, by others.

It got to be four hours . . . five . . . six. What cruel suspense. It would be the same, Anthony realized, in Northampton, for my parents. He phoned them, confirming the suspense: there was no news. Robert Klopstock, who had come from his own day's work as a surgeon in another hospital, joined those who waited. He was able, with authority, to reassure the rest that the absence of news was positive news—it meant that the operation was still proceeding with expectations of success. Anxiety, I gather, seemed more cogent than Robert's reassurances, however. My partners, Frank Patton and Bill Ellis, called and Anthony apprised them of the situation.

Dr. Porter sent a message from the operating room to report to those waiting that in addition to the diagnosed condition, there had been complications encountered, thus ratifying, finally, Dr. Abramson's astute appraisal of several weeks before. Hidden from other means of detection, there was a growth on the pancreas, its rupture imminent; indeed, there was surprise that it had not burst in the recent past, given its location and appearance. Had that happened there could have been no remedy that might be quickly enough administered to save life. Another, less ominous, complication was the spleen, also at the point of rupturing, which had to be removed. (I wondered, when I learned this later, whether the loss of one's spleen would affect one's theology.)

Dr. Porter and his colleagues persevered. Some ten hours after the surgery had begun, it was finished, and Dr. Porter returned to those waiting. "Strange as it may seem," he announced to them, "your friend is alive."

The congregation dispersed, again. Anthony made several telephone calls, and went, then, with Mel Schoonover and Bill Ellis for a drink, and for the first meal he had thought to have that day.

Meanwhile, I had been in oblivion. There is a peculiar injustice in love which casts the more difficult burdens of one's life upon those who love and which frees the beloved. That is how it had been, during the surgery, for those who waited and for me. Sometime toward the next morning I was returned from oblivion. I awoke in the recovery room. I was alive, alright; I could tell that because it hurt. Ferocious pain raged in my body. I tried to touch myself to see how much of my body was there, but I could not find my body. I shuddered hard. I remember speaking the name of Jesus. Then someone was nearby, someone doing something, someone touching me—I could see that, I did not feel anything. And then I was quiet.

When I woke, later, there were three figures in my hospital room. With an effort I focused upon them and recognized James A. Pike and Diane Kennedy and Anthony.

During the vigil, Anthony had received a telephone call at the hospital from Bishop Pike. I had known, and admired, Bishop Pike since 1955, while he was Dean of New York and I was a student at the Harvard Law School, when we had met and had long conversations about theology and law and about being at once a Christian and a lawyer, as both of us were. Subsequently, when I moved to New York and began my East Harlem practice, we became good friends, and colleagues in some issues in the city and in the churches. After he became Bishop of California, we remained in communication. I usually saw him on his whirlwind trips to New York, and I visited him several times in San Francisco. When heresy proceedings were initiated against the bishop, he asked me to be legal counsel and, during the heresy controversy, Harper and Row commissioned Anthony and myself to write *The Bishop Pike Affair*. At the 1967 Seattle General Convention of the Episcopal Church—at which Bishop Pike won vindication on the heresy issues—Diane Kennedy, who was then aiding the bishop in research and writing, and Anthony and I, joined the bishop as an informal caucus concerned with strategy in the debate and disposition of the heresy matter in the House of Bishops. That experience had occasioned our admiration for Diane, and Anthony and I rejoiced to learn later on that Jim and Diane would marry.

The bishop knew that I was ill, that it was serious, that surgery had been considered, but he did not know the extremity that my condition had reached, and he did not know the date that had been set for the operation. Nevertheless, on that day, during the vigil, while the outcome in surgery was dubious, Bishop Pike had somehow managed to locate Anthony at the hospital by telephone. "I had an overwhelming conviction that I should find out what's happening to Bill," he told Anthony. Anthony reported that the operation was happening, that it was continuing much longer than expected, and that he, and others who were waiting, felt grave and uncertain.

Pike had called from Baltimore where he, accompanied by Diane, had been on a lecture engagement. Their plans to travel elsewhere were canceled and they came instead to New York to the hospital and were present when I revived.

Still traumatized, and heavily sedated, I have but one vivid recollection of their visit. There had been some conversation and then, suddenly, as it seemed to me, Pike had exclaimed: "Well, I'm a bishop, I'd better do something." Thereupon he disappeared briefly. He reappeared near the doorway to the room, in the company of my nurse. He had procured from her a large jar of petroleum jelly, which he proceeded to consecrate duly. He admonished the nurse that the substance had now been set apart for uses other than those ordinary and familiar for Vaseline. Taking a thumbful of this freshly made unguent, he came to the bedside and anointed me, signing my forehead with a cross, and saying:

> *I anoint you, in the name of God; beseeching the mercy of our Lord Jesus Christ, that all your pain and sickness of body being put to flight, the blessing of health may be restored unto you. Amen.*

That is, of course, practically verbatim, the unction of the sick prescribed in the Book of Common Prayer.

The following morning Dr. Porter stopped by and he told me in detail what had happened in surgery and what the prognosis was. He was, I noted, since I was now lucid, pleased and proud about the operation, and properly so, for all that it had been a prolonged and exacting work for him. "I don't know whether or not you

178

realize it," he began, "but your recovery is spectacular!"

"That doesn't surprise me at all," I interrupted him. "I was anointed with Vaseline by Bishop Pike—what else would you expect?"

a gift of healing

I had been the beneficiary of another unction. On the day before the operation, following the Eucharist, Ann Thompson had remained after the rest had departed. She and Anthony and I talked for a while, mainly reminiscing about the days when we had lived in New York. Bishop Pike's name was incidentally mentioned in the conversation; Ann had met him one day when he had come to the apartment during the period in which Anthony and I were writing *The Bishop Pike Affair*. Ann had heard uncomplimentary things about Pike and had been glad to meet him and assess him for herself. They had had a substantial conversation over coffee in the kitchen, while Anthony had been working in the study and I had been writing in bed. That is how Pike's name came up in the hospital conversation—we remembered when I had broken my ankle and was immobilized in a cast and, for more than two months, engaged, somewhat awkwardly, in writing my share of the *Pike* book in bed. Ann did much to look after me while I was in the cast and, because of the accident, she and Anthony and I had talked a good deal about accidents and illnesses and healing and health—and what these had to do with the Gospel and the Gospel with them. The writing of the *Pike* manuscript being concurrent with the broken leg meant the three of us also talked of the bishop and, when he visited the household, and she and he became acquainted, Ann liked the bishop. Several other bishops had come to see Anthony and myself during those same months, so that we might hear from them about various aspects of the heresy controversy, as part of our research for the book, and I recall saying, facetiously, to Ann one day, "You'd think, with all the bishops who have been here, one could have healed my ankle." "Oh, no," Ann responded seriously, "*they* don't know about things like that—except for Bishop Pike. *He* knows."

We reminisced about these things until Ann suggested that I should rest. She stood beside the bed; Anthony was at the foot of it; before leaving, she would pray for my life and for my healing, she said. The prayer was spontaneous, fervent, pointed, beautiful. Ann Thompson has authority as a Christian.

A few days later, on an afternoon following surgery, Ann returned to the hospital. She was very glad to hear that Bishop Pike had been there earlier and that he had anointed me, although she seemed not a bit surprised that he

182

had come. It was what she expected of him. We talked briefly, and then Ann prayed, thanking God for the skill and care of the surgeon, doctors, nurses, hospital workers, for the concern and love of others, for the healing which had begun, and for zeal in living.

thorns in the flesh

There had been a return from the threshold
of death, which had been called "spectacular,"
healing had begun; with patience, common
sense and medicine my recuperative prospects
were excellent. Yet death is not merely a destination or state of being, which, for want of
more suitable words, men describe as a place.
It *is* that, alright, and I could readily picture the
course of the illness and what had happened
in surgery as a journey to the site of death.
Death, however, as I have already intimated,
is a moral reality in *this* place—in the world, a
domineering principle in the common existence of human beings and principalities and
all things. If I had not crossed death's threshold,
I was still not absent from the presence of
death, immune from the wiles of death, ignorant of the work of death, or indifferent to the
power of death. If anything, being so spared
from death has made me more acutely aware
of the manifold forms of death and the more
respectful of the moral ubiquity of death.

All of this was made very concrete in the aftermath of surgery, which has left me without the physiological capabilities of naturally furnishing enough enzymes to utilize food and of producing enough insulin to control the body's sugar intake. The necessary removal of diseased and damaged portions of the pancreas, which has both these enzyme and insulin functions, has made me permanently deficient in enzymes and a pseudodiabetic. I had been forewarned of these likely residual liabilities by the surgeon and suffered no surprise that my prognosis was, in these respects, conditional. Both the enzyme deficiency and the diabetes are subject to medical management and while both involve restrictions in diet and activity and personal regime, which a person could happily do without, neither is nor need be disabling in a drastic way. When the time arrived for me to assume responsibility for the daily supervision of my new condition, I had already come to regard it as more of a nuisance than a hindrance.

What did impress me much, rather than the techniques of consuming animal enzymes and injecting insulin in awkwardly located regions of the anatomy, was that these consequences of the operation, which are, in one sense, an advantageous exchange for death, are tangible evidences of the continued vitality of death in the context of my own life. Death may have been, in terms of the illness, foiled or cheated or detoured or put off, but the power of death

had not abandoned me. What particularly
evoked attention, in adjusting to the postopera-
tive realities, is the prominence of time, in relation to death—a matter, it will be recalled,
with which I had struggled during the illness
and about which there had been some insight
on the day previous to surgery. Such is the
juxtaposition of time and death in the kind of
medical control which is prescribed for a person in my health limitations, that neglect or
other inability to follow routine in timely fash-
ion could be fatal. Not only is sudden death a
potentiality, but sustained unpunctuality could
be so debilitating that it eventuates in death.
Beyond the risks of these relatively quick or
slow deaths, time and death are related, in my
circumstances, in another way, that is, morally.
The peril of death is concealed in the issue of
whether a person with such health necessities
is *so* obedient to time that he becomes enslaved
to it, allowing his whole existence to be regi-
mented. If such a person is not able to master
the medical requisites and is, instead, totally
regulated in his life by them, then he becomes
a chronic victim and morally dies. Then, the
very procedures commendable for sustaining
life become radically dehumanizing and the
actual state of the person is the moral equivalent of death. This is a tyranny of time which,
obviously, has close parallels in many jobs and
occupations where men become so intimidated
by schedules and deadlines and temporal pri-

orities that (ironically) they have no time to live humanly and become, as it is said, "as good as dead." My musing in the hospital, as I began to be acquainted with these issues involving time with death in various ways, was refreshed by the prospect that I would be living, and, when the time came, working on Block Island. There is little idolatry of time on the Island, in fact, the prevailing spirit of the community is somewhat contemptuous of time, having more of a sense of history than of destiny, and the style of life there implicitly ridicules the ethics of mainland society which makes men slaves of time. The Island would be a propitious place for my recuperation. No doubt Giselle would discern the providential in the fact that this is where I would return.

Of the two frailties—the enzyme deficiency and the diabetes—the former is the more readily managed and far less erratic. Regulation of the diabetes, as some millions of other American diabetics appreciate and as millions more undetected diabetics need to know, is a delicate and elaborate matter, partly because there is still vast scientific ignorance about it, partly because there are so many variables to cope with, both for a particular diabetic and among diabetics as a class.

The eccentricities of diabetes, and the foibles attending its treatment and management, have occasioned the development of a cultus around the disease which has—I fear—rendered many diabetics vulnerable to exploitations, both economic and psychological. There is a constituency of diabetics in this country who are induced to regard their affliction in pseudoreligious terms, quite similar to the ethos one beholds in havens of fantasy and aberrant religious practice like the Masons or the Eastern Star. The publications of the American Diabetic Association, for a specific example, reek with such overtones. The obscurity of the ailment itself, and the idiosyncracies of the present therapy, lend themselves easily to this cultism. Diabetes and its control involves an array of attributes and practices strikingly parallel to those usually found in organized religion or the secular imitations of religion familiar in fraternal orders. At the center of it is an extraordinary secret, to which only an elect are admitted. There are rites of initiation (an insulin injection), which must, thereafter, be fastidiously repeated (the daily insulin injections), preceded by a purification ceremony (the sterilization of the syringe and swabbing the injection site), together with dietary regulations (the computation of food elements and the preparation of special recipes), times of special obligation (the regularization of medication, meals, exercise and rest). And these ablutions and other rituals are mandatory for the initiated, sanctioned by the threat of punishment in distress, pain or even death (the perpetual risks of insulin shock or diabetic

coma). There are even established congregations or lodges in this cult (the so-called lay
chapters of the American Diabetic Association).

As a diabetic, I can only speak as a novice
(to use the appropriate religious terminology).
I am aware that similar cults exist with respect
to other diseases, but that only fortifies my un-
easiness with the diabetic cult. I suppose such
machinations can be rationalized as uplifting
the morale of diabetics or even as affording an
elementary group therapy. I just say, here, and
for now, that it offends me as a human being
to be addressed as if my diabetes is a mark of
honor or a privilege or a source of special status.
I think that is morbid, infantile and essentially
unhealthy, psychogenically and physiologi-
cally. Diabetics, or those with other diseases or
disabilities in comparable circumstances, who
are induced to become cultists are too vulnerable to commercial exploitation by the health
industry—the medical profession, the pharma-
ceutical business, charities promotions, the
manufacturers and merchandisers of cultus
products. The cult phenomenon is offensive because it leaves adherents *so* defenseless, such
inviting prey, that, in American society it would
be utterly astounding if diabetics are not being
importuned. And the necessary further inference is that conscientious, impartial, non-
commercial research and treatment is, at the

least, retarded or deprived or denied priority
because of the indulgence of the cult.

The diabetes and the enzyme incapacity
were not the only thorns in the flesh in surgery's wake. While in the hospital, and during
convalescence on the Island, there were other
signs of the vigor and persistence of death. In
a succession that seemed to me remarkable, a
number of persons, some of them close associates, all of them men who had swayed my
thinking and conduct, all with whom I felt
specially identified, died. Karl Barth's death
was among these. So was the death of Norman
Thomas, whom I had first met more than
twenty years ago and with whom I had occasional conversations, particularly about the
ethics of social change. Thomas, it will be recalled, occupied his first and only pulpit at the
Church of the Ascension in East Harlem and
that fact had been an encouragement to me
when I worked, much later, in the same neighborhood. Brooks Quimby died within days of
Barth and Thomas. A professor at Bates College, where I had been an undergraduate, he
had a dogged passion for ascertaining the facts
and a fierce integrity in expounding his convictions (with which I, mainly, disagreed); he
was, easily, the most influential teacher of my
experience. Then there was the bizarre accident in Bangkok that killed Thomas Merton.
He had been glad about *My People Is the Enemy* and from that a communication between

us had developed. Twice arrangements had been made to meet at the monastery in Kentucky where he lived and twice my illness had thwarted our intentions. I regretted this, as Merton did, although I do not honestly think that our communication was diminished just because we did not meet. A few weeks later, news reached Block Island that Ralph McGill was dead. We had met in Atlanta. I revered him, intuiting that he was some kind of patriarch. Hoping for an untroubled convalescence, I had agreed to go on Good Friday, 1969, to Atlanta to preach the traditional three-hour meditation on the last words from the cross at the congregation of which McGill was a communicant. I wished much to be able to do this, partly because the event was to be in Atlanta and that date would be the first anniversary of Dr. King's assassination, as well as a more ancient anniversary, and also because it would mean a conversation with Ralph McGill.

"All of my heroes are dying," I remarked to Anthony, ruefully. It was not so much any one of these deaths by itself, though each man was mourned for himself, but the association of these deaths in time, the gathering of the deaths of these men together, which troubled me and challenged me. I thought about this succession of deaths, now and again, in the months of recuperation. That they represented further tokens of death's power, as if any more were needed, was plain enough, but I was vaguely conscious of there being some other connection amongst those who had died and between them and myself. For a while I could not quite grasp it or articulate it, but I nevertheless knew it to be a vocational connection.

The matter at last took focus because of another death of another man whose life I affirmed in the same way as the others: James Pike. No doubt the interval between the day Pike was known to be lost in the desert and the discovery of his body caused me to concentrate upon the issue of that vocational connection. Then, too, the congregation at Saint Clement's Church in New York City asked if I would preach at their Requiem for Bishop Pike, and the preparation of that homily proved to be edifying. What is connective in all of these deaths and my own life has nothing, as such, to do with imitating the work of any of these men or any efforts to continue their tasks, their ideas, their concerns, but that does have everything to do with vocation, with vocation as each of them exemplified vocation, with my vocation, with the vocation to which all men are called, with the vocation of living as a human being. There is the ubiquity and tenacity of death, but there is in the midst of that reality, the continuity and continuance of life. Curiously, but also appropriately, as Anthony mentioned after the service at Saint Clement's, the preparation and utterance of the homily commending James Pike was the first work that I had been enabled to do, since the surgery, about which I had vocational conviction. I had recuperated.

the rumor of miracles

In the weeks at Columbia-Presbyterian, and
during the months in convalescence, in a recovery which at times seemed as gradual and
reluctant as the disease had been unremitting
and relentless, I brooded over the dialectic of
prayer and healing, the intercourse of faith and
health, the relation of the gift of love to the
event of living. I had received Ann Thompson's
healing intercessions, the unction bestowed by
Bishop Pike, the Holy Communion in that remarkable congregation in which Bishop Wetmore had been celebrant. I had benefited from
the providential encounter of Dr. Porter, suffered an acceptance of my vocation in the recall of my past, and been supported patiently
in my household, considerately by Island neighbors, earnestly by a community more widespread. My mind mulled over all these things:
each, somehow, I knew, impinged upon both
survival and recovery: each, somehow, had to
do with being healed.

195

As if to emphasize the abundance of my blessings, I had also known rejection during the illness and in its aftermath. The story, in its details, I forebear to confide. Suffice to say that there is a person, welcomed into my life, before the illness was evident, as a friend, who, upon beholding my disease, abhorred me rather than the disease, and literally fled from my presence. It bugged me a lot. It engaged me in a mighty struggle within my being to accept this rejection and not reciprocate bitterly. It required my penance. The experience is, I suppose, not exceptional in a culture so cosmetically oriented as this, where value is attributed to appearances, where packaging rather than contents procures buyers, where the pretenses of youth and health are so assiduously maintained. In any case, I had not recognized this issue at firsthand before. The person—perceiving the extremity of my ailment, visibly unnerved by my pain and patently demoralized by my emaciation—had concluded, logically, that I was dying and that dead, I was useless. Not that my death was the person's desire, there was no meanness in it, it is just that my condition was assumed to have altered our relationship into a morbid obligation. It is only that there was a misapprehension of love mixed up with an apprehensiveness of loving. And so there was panic, there was a terrifying necessity to terminate contact, there was an urgency to escape. Perchance what could be seen in my appearance anticipated

too clearly my acquaintance's own death. If
that be so, it is pathetic, since there is no place
to hide from the presence of death. Perhaps
that is, by now, appreciated, somewhat, by the
one who ran away. I do know that the news
of my survival provoked astonishment and agi-
tation. Maybe, however, the confusion has sub-
sided and it is now acknowledged that death is
not so much to fear.

My meditations—as recuperation began—on
all that had happened were haunted by the
problem of miracles and the radical ambiguities
attending that subject. Giselle, who is a poetess,
readily invoked the word *miracle* in speaking
of the crisis on November 22. Anthony, a poet,
did too. I found that the word did not so readily come from my lips and I turned to another
poet, W. H. Auden, whose father was a physician and who wrote "Healing . . . is not a science but the intuitive art of wooing Nature."
I did not have confidence I understood that,
either, but the statement's ambiguity was less
intimidating to me than the explicit language
of miracles. I might have suppressed the issue
by classifying the problem of miracles as only
a concern of poetry. Auden, in the same poem
cited, does something of the sort:

> *"Every sickness*
> *is a musical problem,"*
> *so said Novalis,*
> *"and every cure*
> *a musical solution"*

I could not do that, however, if only because others, who are not poets, were saying the same thing, or, at least, using the same word, *miracle*, in reference to my survival and prospective recovery. Dr. Klopstock (perhaps in deference to Giselle, I could not tell) was one of these; Mel Schoonover, who has a particular authority as a Christian on matters of illness and healing because of his own exceptional history, was another; after I returned to the Island, I heard Dr. Katherine Breydert, a retired physician and a most sophisticated Christian theologically, one of our neighbors there, speak in a similar way. Will Campbell, a true preacher, who drove up from Nashville to see me in the hospital, had mentioned resurrection in a way that was related somehow to the subject. Stan Newman, who brought news and greetings from the Chicago black ghetto where he works, was unabashed about it. Ann Thompson could say *miracle* so matter-of-factly that it did not startle me. But having Bengt greet me, gruffly, with, "I didn't think I'd see you again. It's a miracle!" gave me pause. My father, who resigned to the likelihood of my death as if it were yet another indignity that a father must bear who has a son who never follows his advice, had, I think, alluded to miracles when he told me: "You're damn lucky, do you know that?"

I recognized, of course, a semantic issue here. A term was being used in different senses, with different subtleties, to some extent, for different purposes. Still, semantic ambiguity did not dismiss my question about what had happened to me or how it might, decently, be designated. I recognized, indeed, that decency was a prime influence in my reticence in speaking of miracles generally and in my instinctive reserve in hearing of my own experience categorized in such a way.

More specifically, there is the problem created by those who prey upon the sick while professing magical healing capabilities, and there is the presence of the many in the fold of the churches in whom an essentially superstitious attitude about healing (as about prayer) has been instilled. I refer to the likes of Oral Roberts, whom I regard as a superlative flimflam man, and the likes of Norman Vincent Peale who is, as I have said before, most appropriately classified as a sorcerer. Having fathomed their disguises, I would not abet charlatans or witches, and I would not want to, even inadvertently, mislead the superstitious since they are so mercilessly exploited in the churches. During convalescence, there have been overtures to engage in either. My illness had been reported in some newspapers and in the religious journals, and there had been gossip about it on the grapevines of Christendom. In consequence I was importuned by certain non-medical "healers," making grandiose claims of conjuring powers, seeking the loan of my

name and my body, and, most of all, my conscience, to their enterprises.

This is why to write about my own illness
and surgery and, particularly, to write about
my own survival when death had been expected, seemed initially a vain and macabre
venture. When suggested to me by Bengt, I
ridiculed the thought—summoning to my argument recollections of Lyndon Johnson dis-
playing his gall bladder wound to photogra-
phers and of those technicolor prints of kidney
operations to which *Life* magazine sometimes
resorts. I am no exhibitionist and I had no wish
to add to curious entertainments. Besides, to
have pain, even for a very long time and even
in unremittent intensity, is not, as I have
learned, especially noteworthy. Healing is a
splendid mystery—though no greater a mystery
than love—and its dignity ought not to be vul-
garized.

Most church people, to mention no others,
I am afraid, have become so unbiblical in their
minds that they think miracle means magic, and
they seem to suffer fakers and fools gladly, at
least they patronize them in various ways even
when the hocus-pocus is ostentatious and trans-
parent, even where obvious commercial advan-
tage is taken, or even, sometimes, where a
disavowal of legitimate medical practice is involved. Church people are often so deeply im-
bued with a fairy-tale version of the Gospel,
from the corruptions of Sunday school and the

like, that they would rather be conned than relinquish their fables.

I was bothered to hear so many who are close to me and who had known of the crisis in my health invoke the language of miracles about my healing. I would not have volunteered that name myself just because of the false connotation of supernatural tricks attached to it. There was no miracle in any sense such as that in my being healed.

Still, I knew that miracle is a more versatile symbol which can be meant without gainsaying the arts of surgeons and physicians and without real comparison to the business of conjurers or the doctrine of wizards. I realized that what miracle signified to all who had invoked it about my survival was a gratitude for my recovery from death. They bespoke the splendor of the mysteries of healing and of love.

When all due allowances have been made for doctors and for medicine, it is when these mysteries—healing and love—are joined that, in fact, a miracle happens.

What is involved, then, whatever else is implicated, is self-love. The love of others is there, but that alone can not suffice, as potent as it may be. Self-love is decisive. I do not mean, by that, a strenuous will to live. I refer to a reality which is, indeed, rather the opposite: a love of self which, esteeming life itself as a gift, expects or demands no more than the life which is given, and which welcomes and embraces and affirms that much unconditionally. I mean self-love which emulates, and, in the end, participates in, the love of God for life.

The evening next after my return to the Island from the hospital, Anthony and Bengt and I had a meal together. It was an unexpected celebration. It recalled for all of us the meal we had shared just before I left the Island to enter the hospital. That previous meal was similar to a wake. My friends were both persuaded it was the last time we would have a meal together. They were prematurely mourning. I had my accustomed distress from the illness, but I did not have their apprehension and my morale was good.

It was during the second meal that Bengt first pressed the idea of writing this book. He insisted it need not be morbid or grisly or vain. "We were both sure that you would die," he mentioned the other meal, "but you didn't feel that way that night." Bengt has a habit of protesting a lack of sophistication whenever he is about to say something truly sophisticated. "I am just a seaman," he continued, "but I think it was faith. I call that faith. You had faith." It seemed an accusation. "You have to write about faith."

Well, one can write of faith and, thus, as here, speak of prayer and providence, vocation and freedom from time, work and dominion, recall and absolution, healing and love, the transcendence of death in many ways and eucharist for life. Or, one can be succinct: life is a gift which death does not vitiate or void: faith is the acceptance, honoring, rejoicing in that gift. That being so, in my own story, *it did not matter whether I died*. Read no resignation or indifference into this confession. It is freedom from moral bondage to death that enables a man to live humanly and to die at any moment without concern.

Or, forsaking words, one can act, that is, anyway, a plainer way to speak.

On Block Island, it is a custom for folk to name their homes. Sometime after immigrating to the Island, I had obtained a sign which I intended to put up for this purpose, but I had not done so. First thing, the morning after that second meal with Bengt and Anthony, I mounted the sign upon the gatepost.

On the sign is the name of home: ESCHA-TON. It is a message for Bengt—and for everyone else.

After graduating from Harvard Law School, **William Stringfellow** decided to set up a free practice on "the poorest block in Harlem." He described his seven years there in the pioneering book on race relations *My People Is The Enemy*.

After leaving Harlem Mr. Stringfellow made himself widely known as a writer and lecturer, and gained prominence as an Episcopal lay theologian and as a leader among the social critics of our times. He is a frequent guest on TV and radio programs, and has been described by *Time* magazine as "one of Christianity's most persuasive critics from within."

3

Date Due

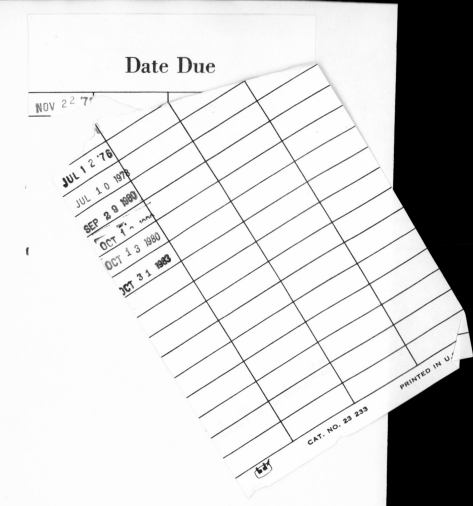